WINIFRED: A WILTSHIRE WORKING GIRL

Front cover: Winifred, about 1918
Back cover: Winifred 1990, with Suzanne Lenglen's racquet

Winifred Grace in 1991

Winifred

A Wiltshire Working Girl

*Her Childhood on Salisbury Plain
and early working life in Berkshire
as told to Sylvia Marlow*

EX LIBRIS PRESS

Published in 1991 by
Ex Libris Press
1 The Shambles
Bradford on Avon
Wiltshire

Typeset in 11 point Palatino
Printed by BPPC Wheatons Ltd., Exeter

ISBN 0 948578 27 0

To Winifred, of course, with love

Contents

Acknowledgements

I should like to thank the Bodleian Museum for access to Parliamentary Papers and Agricultural Returns, and the following for kind permission to refer to their work: N.D.G. James (*Plain Soldiering*), Mr. A.Edwards (*Everleigh — some notes on its story* by W.A.Edwards), G.E.Mingay and Messrs Heinemann (*Rural Life in Victorian England*).

Photographs are reproduced by kind permission of Newbury District Museum, Wiltshire Archaelogical and Natural History Society, Wiltshire Library and Museum Service, Mr. N.D.G.James, Mrs. Sue Hopson, Mrs. Anne Beese, Mr. A.P.Baggs and Mrs.P.Colman F.R.S.A., Dip.LLH to all of whom I am most grateful.

I also thank Wiltshire County Council Local Studies Library and Wiltshire Record Office for their help at various stages.

My warmest thanks go to Winifred without whose inspiration, trust and enthusiasm nothing could have been done, to Christopher Marlow who unfailingly encouraged and provided indispensable practical help, and to Roger Jones, my long suffering publisher.

FOREWORD by Pamela Street

As Sylvia Marlow so rightly says in her Introduction to *Winifred — a Wiltshire Working Girl*, there is today an ever-growing desire to learn about the past from the words of those who lived through it. This short book is the perfect answer to that need. Would that there were more historians willing to take the trouble to record first-hand accounts of 'ordinary' people — in this instance, one of the daughters of a farm labourer and his wife who was brought up on Salisbury Plain in the early part of the century.

What comes over on every page is the poverty, privation and sheer grit which helped the family survive against appalling odds. One did not bemoan one's lot, one just got on with it — even though a childless lady from a nearby large house wanted to adopt Winifred. Always eager for life, the young girl sometimes regretted that her mother had refused this request and therefore, in consequence, she was deprived of finding out more about the world.

Sylvia Marlow is to be congratulated on the way she has marshalled her material, standing back from the story and letting Winifred speak for herself, so that the reader becomes increasingly interested in her and is anxious for her ultimate well-being.

It was the importance of learning about lives such as Winifred's and not simply those of the famous which inspired the late Sir Arthur Bryant to become an historian. At an early age he transcribed some letters he had accidentally come across, which had been written in the seventeenth century. 'As

I worked on them,' he wrote, 'I could hear the whispering voices of men and women who, after the silence of centuries had found a listener and were trying to speak ... Here were real lives that had once meant as much to their possessors as mine to me ... the stuff of which history is made.'

Happily, thanks to the aid of the modern tape recorder and the skill and dedication of Sylvia Marlow, we have not had to wait quite so long to be put into this particular and valuable picture.

Pamela Street, 1991

INTRODUCTION

Until recent times history has been presented mainly in terms of major world events and the doings of the great. But what of the "ordinary" people on whose lives those events impinged? How were they affected and what did they, the majority, feel about the world they lived in? Today there is a growing sense that our perception and understanding of the past can be enriched by access to oral testimony from those who lived through it. Oral History enthusiasts are now encouraging us to listen to stories about the recent past; to ask how folk lived and worked, what joys and sorrows they experienced; and, with the permission of the tellers, to record and store these memories before they are lost to us.

I had known Mrs. Winifred Grace slightly for a number of years before I thought of asking her about her life in the early years of this century. I knew that she and her husband had come to her present Buckinghamshire village in 1954, both working into their seventies, and that he died in 1973. I also knew that she had a fund of memories dating from her childhood in rural Wiltshire.

In the late 1980's I took to visiting her regularly and began to hear stories of a time, a way of living and a part of England unfamiliar to me. I learned how hard a cowman had to work in 1900 to earn ten shillings a week and some of the hazards of living in tied cottages. I heard in detail how harvesting and haymaking were carried out in the days before mechanisation. Every so often my ear was delighted by a regional word or phrase — "skillins", "kevins", "pook it up".

All this seemed too valuable to be lost and, with Winifred's permission, I began to tape record our conversations. Later I would transcribe and read them over and see whether we could re-create her life. What resulted is in these pages, neither biography nor autobiography, but a true story put together from spoken recollections.

Winifred's memory for the broad sequence of events and for precise details — such as the exact day, month and year she entered domestic service — was excellent and I soon had on tape a factual account in everyday language of her childhood, early youth, marriage and life up to the present. However, in some ways I felt that I had only the skeleton of a life. This was what people did, this was what happened to them, but how did they express themselves, how did they *feel* about everything? The answer seemed to be that endurance required a stoicism and a kind of grit that could not coexist with sentiment. In Winifred's words "You just got on with it." The starkness, the lack of ornament in her telling meant that the facts would have largely to speak for themselves.

Gradually though, as we covered some areas a second or third time, episodes filled out and acquired colour. Sometimes a gem of information would emerge on a day when I was without my machine and I would scribble a note rather than lose it.

We persevered through some twenty tapes, at intervals chatting over photographs and newspaper cuttings she had kept. A picture of the Spencer family gradually emerged: an iron-willed mother, a soft-hearted father, young Winifred and her brother Ted. Sisters, much older, dropped in and out of the story from time to time. I was disappointed not to have gained a clearer impression of their individual characters. Shadowy figures, they are all gone now, and with them any secrets of their pleasures, pains, loves, hopes and fears.

Home for the Spencers was an isolated cottage in the heart of Salisbury Plain, a world where everything that lived and grew had value. The children were taught to wrest every scrap of benefit from their environment. They plundered the meadows and hedgerows for mushrooms and raspberries. They went after plovers' eggs, climbed trees for rooks' eggs, even sparrows could be snared for a pie. Not a weed was wasted if the family pig could eat it, not a tuft of sheep's wool left on a fence if their Mother could spin and knit it up. While their father often trapped wild animals, she took charge of the domestic ones, a vital source of nourishment.

Thrifty as she was and intent on her family's survival, Winifred's mother maintained a scrupulous regard for the rights of others and for natural laws: racing pigeons found in her barn were faithfully restored to their owners; the pig, chickens and goats that served the family so well must in their turn be decently housed and cared for.

In sharp contrast was Winifred's evocation of domestic service in a small Berkshire town: the Home Front during the First World War, with its privations and losses; the jealous hierarchies among servants; the off-duty delights of fairs, fêtes and the silent cinema.

Eventually I began the task of ordering the transcribed material and putting it into readable form. My starting point was the residual Spencer family of four, the pattern of their days and the incidents that very occasionally punctuated them. This first part formed itself most naturally into a loose combination of background and topics. When it came to reproducing the world of wage earning, responsibility and the shocks of premature adulthood a slightly more formal narrative seemed appropriate. I used this for Parts II and III, ending, as we had agreed, with the marriage in 1924 .

These three parts embody the substance of conversations recorded as I have described — sorted out, pruned here, re-shaped there but containing nothing fictitious. Nothing, that is, except the names of one location and five people. In three cases this was to protect anonymity, in the others the original names have been forgotten. Much of what Winifred told me appears verbatim in the text. Where this was not possible I hope her own voice comes through in the telling.

I have verified a number of dates and other details, partly

to avoid confusion and partly out of personal interest. However, no claims are made for historical, topographical or agricultural accuracy. Essentially matters are recorded as they appeared in the eyes of a child and later a young woman and as they were recalled seventy or eighty years later. This may not always coincide with factual reports.

I am glad to have a record of this life — courageous, often thwarted, deeply human. Those times have slipped away, those places are irrevocably changed, but the tale is there to enrich our perception and understanding. What for me is moving is the yearning, questing, battling spirit that transcends the everyday language:

> I didn't want a drab life, I wanted to *do* things, make things, read, find out about the world, learn how all sorts of things were made, learn about the past — history — and most of all I wanted to learn music and play the piano.

The spirit in that child has never died.

Sylvia Marlow
Oving, Bucks.
April 1991

*Full many a flower is born to blush unseen
And waste its sweetness on the desert air.*

Gray's Elegy

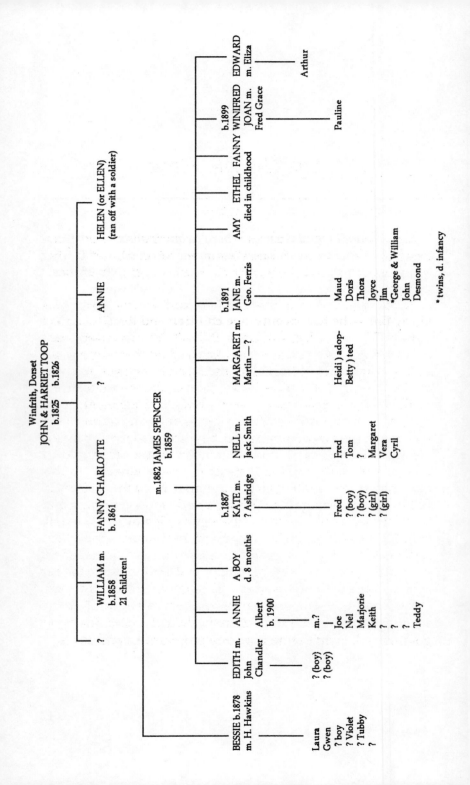

Life On The Plain

I never saw my grandparents but I remember the postman bringing a letter to say Mother's mother had died, and Mother being upset because she wouldn't be able to get to the funeral in Dorset.

Mother had four or five brothers and sisters. There was Uncle Bill — he had twenty-one children and lived to a good old age. There's still one of Uncle Bill's children lives between Swindon and Devizes, as far as I know. And then there was a young sister, rather like me, Mother used to say, and this was the baby sister Mother was always talking about – Aunt Helen, or Ellen. Aunt Helen was a very pretty girl, engaged to the village carpenter at Winfrith. He got a cottage and done it out for her and they were supposed to be going to marry. Well, she went to a dance, I don't know whether it was at Weymouth or where, but Mother did talk about it, how she went to this dance and met a soldier, an artilleryman. Now the artillery in full dress uniform got that lovely braid and everything and there he was in all his glory, all his glory. Mother used to talk about it, how Aunt Helen went with him and married him. She packed a few things and the next day they found she'd gone. She never once wrote home and they never saw her again. That's why my mother was so down on soldiers. And there was Aunt Annie. I can remember 'cause Aunt Annie swallowed a plum stone and then she died of cancer. She never got married. I can't remember any more uncles and aunts.

I was Mother's twelfth child and her eleventh girl. She never really wanted girls — well, it was such a worry when they had to work away from home, what might happen to them — but she was unlucky with boys. She had a boy between, I think, Annie and Kate, a beautiful baby they said, but he died at eight months from being vaccinated. A clot came on top of his head and he died of that. Then I was born I was a twin, but my twin was born dead and that was a boy. After me came Ted and at last Mother had her boy, but he was very delicate. She was forty-two then and she had a bad time. After that she had 'misses.'

That made thirteen of us born alive, but the three girls just before me — Amy, Ethel and Fanny — died of diphtheria. Then when I was born, the lady from the big house at Burbage (I think Mother said it was Lady Savernake) wanted to adopt me as she had no children of her own. Mother said No — well, she'd just lost those three — but she said the lady could name me and that's why I'm Winifred Joan.

I always said Mother made a big mistake, not letting me go. Think of all the things I might've done — had a good education, been able to play the piano, learn about all the things I was interested in, travel. Specially as my Mother always said I wasn't meant for work — and all because I didn't like scrubbing floors!

I was born in Burbage but we left there when I was five months old and went to Coombe Bake[1] on Salisbury Plain, three miles from the village of Enford.

Father was taken on as head cowman at Coombe Farm. He got ten shillings a week and our tied cottage. The farmer, Mr. Eustace Maton, was very rich and thought himself quite "the gentleman". He did have a big staff to do everything: a secretary, a man that did keep all the accounts — going out and incoming — then there was the foreman and all the workers under him. There was a Mrs. Maton and I remember a funny thing about her. She was always trying to stop her husband having a bath ... he used to get the copper filled but she would go and put the fire out. Why on earth, I wonder, but people those days didn't seem to think they needed a bath (not like later when the men came home from the War, full of dirt and lice from the trenches.)

Mr. Maton ploughing, pictured in Daily Mirror *January 1917*

They had one daughter, Winifred like me and about my age. One day she came up to Coombe Bake with her father and saw Jinny, my nanny goat. She asked "Papa" if she could have the goat and of course she had to have it. I didn't cry — 'course not, we didn't have to cry; if she wanted the goat, well, the goat went, that was all. I think she soon got tired of it.

Our cottage was stone with a slate roof, quite big, with three bedrooms, living room and kitchen. My elder sisters had all left home by the time we came to Coombe Bake, and it was only Mother, Dad, Maggie, Jane and me, and later Ted. So three bedrooms was enough. (Not like at Burbage ... pretty crowded there, with two or three to a bed, until Father made space by building an extra room over the wellhouse.)

The upstairs floor at Coombe Bake was wood, covered with the rag rugs Mother and Dad used to make. After Maggie and Jane'd left, Ted had his own little room and I had mine, now with a larger than usual bed all to myself. If a sister came for a holiday I shared it with her again.

In my parents' bedroom was a chest of drawers, a wash-

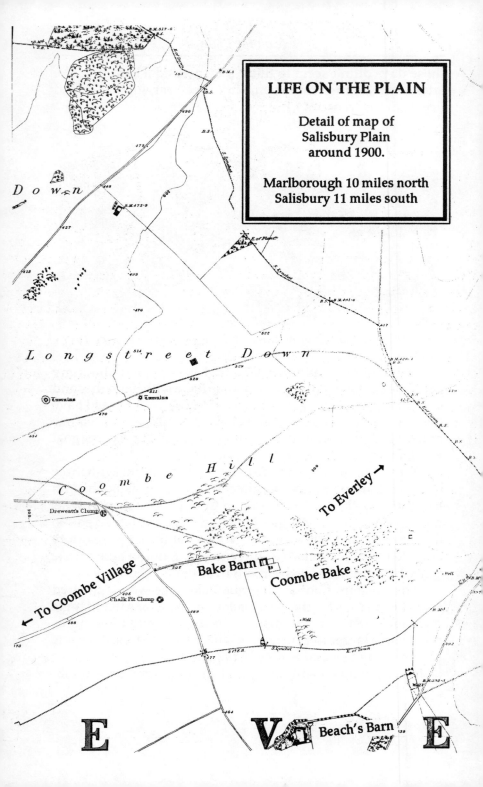

LIFE ON THE PLAIN

Detail of map of
Salisbury Plain
around 1900.

Marlborough 10 miles north
Salisbury 11 miles south

Down

Longstreet Down

Tumulus

Tumulus

Coombe Hill

Dreweatt's Clump

To Everley →

← To Coombe Village

Bake Barn

Coombe Bake

Chalk Pit Clump

E

V

Beach's Barn

E

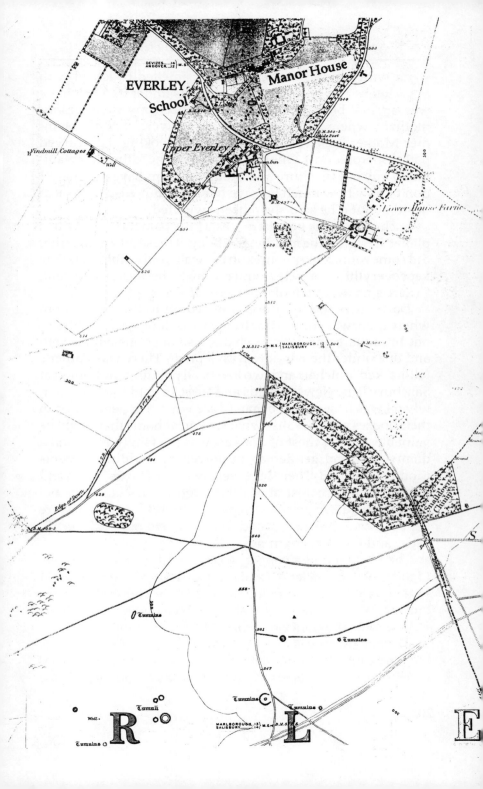

stand with jug and basin, a black enamelled bedstead with brass knobs and of course chamber pots under it. Then there was an oak blanket chest that had been my great-grandmother's where all the winter woollies were stored in summer. Mother kept it polished and I loved looking at the carved pattern of roses on it. One day someone came to the door wanting to buy old furniture and Mother let him have the chest. I don't know how much he gave her for it, but when the Vicar heard about it he said she'd been swindled.

Each side of the bed there was a little bamboo table with a plaited design in the middle. She bought these off a pedlar that did come round. No pictures on the walls, only Bible texts. She kept everything very clean and partickler because, as she said, "There's no need to look poor even if you are."

Downstairs the front door opened on to the living room where there was coconut matting on the floor. Three tables — one big square one with six chairs, a smaller one with a cloth and one under the window with a plant. There was Father's tall-backed armchair and two lovely oil paintings he bought at Salisbury Fair, views of fields and trees, in gold frames. Later, when I was in service, I began to see what rich people had in their houses and to realise what we had at home that might be valuable. On the chest of drawers was the family Bible and a dainty lady and gentleman in porcelain, wedding presents Mother treasured. Then there were two snuff boxes, Ted's and mine. The tobacconist at Marlborough gave them to us because, he said, we were "such dear little children." They were kept one each side of the black box that held our birth certificates, and I've still got mine.

The kitchen had a copper, a range and grate with a hob. Lighting was by oil lamps and candles, and for water we went to the well down the field; rainwater we collected in tubs outside. We was always perished with cold in the winter but no-one took any notice or expected any different.

Outside there was a big vegetable garden behind the cottage and round the front Mother grew asters, stocks and her favourite chrysanths. From my youngest days I had a great love of flowers and it was me that planted the daffodil and tulip bulbs round our home. I got them from the Manor House at Everleigh, the next village. This is how I did it. At the back of the Manor garden was a big yew tree and its branches hung well down over the outside of the wall. There was one stout enough to swing on and I used to swing myself up on to the wall and have a look into the garden. One day I saw a lot of bulbs all dug up and left in a heap. I jumped down and gathered all the bulbs into my pinafore. Then I heard a shout from the head gardener so I grabbed the branch, pulled like mad and swung myself back on to the wall and ran off home. Dad heard about this next time he went drinking at the Crown and then Mother told me off for stealing. She didn't stop me planting the bulbs though!

Tucked away at the back of our cottage, carefully hidden by bushes Mother had planted, was what we called "up the garden" — that was the toilet.

Besides having the cattle to see to, Father had to help out with anything else that wanted doing on the farm. Mother did too, and in between having babies she always milked cows morning and evening, goats too. She'd milked cows ever since she was eight years old and she was very used to them. But I never got used to them, and even now I wouldn't go into a field with them. I've always thought they don't like my smell. Or perhaps it's because of some'ing happened when I was quite small. We were in a field of steers and Mother called me to come to the other side where she was; I went to cross but they trampled me down. The doctors say now that it must have split a nerve in my face and I still sometimes get this funny feeling around my cheekbone.

Mother and Dad had to think of every penny. He had only the ten shillings and we were brought up to understand from the start that we each had to earn our living or starve. It was taken for granted that as each girl got to be twelve or thirteen she would have to go into service. I was the only one to stay at school till fourteen.

21

Mother and Home

If anyone knocks at the door and asks for a cup of water or a crust you must always give it to them — it might be Jesus Christ in disguise.

Mother herself was certainly a good neighbour. I remember a time when a baby was expected in the nextdoor cottage and she went in to help. The midwife from Netheravon came in her pony trap, but soon went off again saying the child was "no bigger'n a pint cup ... won't live." Mother looked at the tiny girl and wondered.

"Well, she's crying ... she's breathing all right ... looks perfect ... and after all, it's a baby ..."

She wrapped her in a warm shawl, brought her into our cottage and started giving her goats' milk every two hours with a drop of brandy. And when the nurse came again the nextdoor baby was doing fine. She got a big surprise — so did Ted and I 'cause we thought she'd be bringing another new baby in the trap!

Now, that nextdoor family emigrated to Canada, but during the Second World War a hospital matron called one day to see Mother. This matron said she'd been taken to Canada as a baby, she was the baby Mother had saved with goats' milk and she'd come to thank her!

Then there was the time Mother rescued three starving children. We were all out in the field one day and we heard crying and a little voice saying, "Emmy, why don't you talk?" coming from down the bottom of the field. Mother went down and found this Emmy, a tall girl about twelve, had fainted and it was her little brother and sister crying. Their parents had locked them in their cottage at Beach's Barn and gone off and left them. Emmy had given most of the food that was left to the little ones and that's why she fainted in our field, coming over to ask for help. They'd climbed out of a window at the back of the cottage. Mother took them home, warmed them by the fire and fed them. Then in the morning she took them in the trap to the police station at Netheravon. They found the parents in the end.

My mother was a good, upright, hard-working, strong-minded woman; severe with us, yes, and did things that today sound hard and unkind; but she felt she had to prepare us for the dangers of a harsh world. We had to be shown the right road, work hard and learn to go without. We must respect the rich, she said, because they provided employment; not envy anyone, say our prayers and ask God to keep us from bad deeds.

She didn't believe in kissing and cuddling. She did say. "That sorta thing leads to other things, "and when I grew up and got engaged I was the same, I could never do all that cuddling and going on. I never had that experience. Mother was very strict about Ted and me not undressing in front of one another. And Father left all that side of things to her, the bringing up. You see when you had a tied cottage you always had to be very careful about how you and your children behaved, specially daughters. Girls in service was always getting into trouble because p'raps the mistress might say to her husband "I'm not having any more children – you must go where you like," and then he might go for the housemaid. Then if she had a baby the family at home would be turned out by the farmer. That's why it was such a worry having all those daughters, and it was never out of Mother's mind.

The work she got through! For twenty years there was nearly always a baby in the cot and the cows to be milked, goats too, chickens and ducks to be fed, and any other jobs that cropped up around the farm. Sometimes she did housework for the Matons for sixpence a day, then she'd be working outside till eight o'clock at night, then supper to get, us to be put to bed, then washing or ironing. She and Dad usually went to bed at nine, but sometimes she was hanging clothes on the line at two in the morning, and sometimes I don't think she went to bed at all.

We worked and lived off the land; not off money but off

everything around us, and making do. We had to do all kinds of things to keep going in the winter else we would have starved. And children had to help, however young we were. When we came home from school in summer time there might be wild raspberries to pick around the Plain; if it was spring we'd be sent to hunt for plovers' eggs. You'd find the nests in open ground, collect the eggs, then leave a stick in the ground so you could find the nest again when they'd laid some more. These eggs were too valuable for the family to keep and they had to go up to the Crown Hotel in Everleigh. The money we got for this went to Mother of course. Other eggs we could get were pigeons', and rooks' — I'd climb trees for these, they tasted good. We never thought of raiding birds' nest in play; everything was serious and to do with work. (I won't say I never found some fun of my own though.)

At haymaking the mowers never cut the grass right up to the hedge. A mass of juicy weeds and nettles would be left and we'd be gathering these for our pig to enjoy. Or after the corn had been cut we'd go leazing for leftover bits of grain. Mother collected it in a jar until there was enough to go to the mill to be ground.

Even if Mother never put us to work Mr. Maton would. Some time after Maggie and Jane had gone into service he was saying to Dad, "Where's those two big girls of yours?" "They're gone into service." "Well, you've got two more, haven't you?" And after that Ted and I were his cheap labour, tugging the docks out of his corn in the light evenings. Cheap labour? Free, wasn't it?

Mother was a great one with her needle — sewing, knitting and crocheting. Women often asked her to make the white calico bonnets they wore in the fields, with the three cords sewn on top, as the custom was. As for knitting, another of our jobs was getting bits of wool for her — off the fences where the sheep had left it. She did twist all these bits up together and pull them into one thread on a hand spindle. She dyed this wool black with the juice from elderberries or blackberries, knitted it up into black stockings for us — and later the stockings might be unpicked to make some'ing else! I hated wearing those stockings, they were so coarse they made my legs itch.

Once Father was in real need of a pair of trousers for the cold winter days on the hills, but he never got the trousers because we needed warm boots for school, so Mother said I must patch up his old trousers. Nothing was ever wasted; if Father's long pants were wore out, they'd be cut up to make warm knickers for me. She used every bit she could, and she and Father often sat making rag rugs out of old clothes in the evenings. She never let any of us off — no good saying you didn't feel like it. I suppose it was good bringing up, because we always knew where we were, that you don't get anything for nothing, that we had to grow up to earn our living.

She always put food first, clothes second; as she said, you can't work without fuel. And we could live rich off the land! Having chickens meant there might be egg for breakfast; Father could have bacon in his sandwiches because we kept a pig. In the evening there would be a stew or a pie, rabbit perhaps or rook pie. People often shot the young rooks, and if you put a bit of bacon with the breast you'd have a lovely supper. Then there was pigeon and sparrow pies sometimes. We had pigeons in the barn — not too many because they're destructive — fantails, white ones and sometimes racing birds would get in there. If a racing pigeon had the owner's name and address on its ring Mother was always careful to write and tell them where it was, and she'd keep the bird for them, if not — pigeon pie!

We never caught blackbirds, thrushes or any songbirds, but we were encouraged to get sparrows and there were scores of them. Often in icy, snowy weather we'd put bread down outside the kitchen door. Sparrows would come — then we dropped a net on them. You may think it was cruel but remember these birds would tear the thatch off a rick and get to work on the corn if they had the chance.

In these ways Mother saw we got some meat to put with the vegetables Father grew.

Something else she kept was bees, not like they are today but in round hives. When she'd got the honey out of the combs she did keep the combs for to make furniture polish. She'd leave so much honey for the bees for the winter and then they'd have to start again. She could sell the honey and beeswax in Marlborough.

She was very clever with hens (and now you'll hear how she wasn't quite perfect!) I remember one day we'd been over to Collingbourne to see my married sister Nell and we were passing by Mr. Nuth's farm at Everleigh. Mr. Nuth had these special hens — Leghorns.

"H'm said Mother. "I'd like a setting of those eggs."

She got out of the trap and went into the rickyard. (They did put the hens there to pick up all the bits of corn — they wouldn't have to feed them then.) Mr. Nuth didn't seem to be around.

"H'm yes, half a dozen, and I can pop them under my broody hens."

She worked out that if she could get a cockerel out of that setting she'd get better layers. You see, she had big heavy Rhodes hens that go broody, and if you have only broody hens you don't get the eggs. Now the Leghorns never go broody so if she put a Leghorn cock with her Rhodes hens she'd have more eggs.

Sure enough she did get two cockerels out of the six eggs, and four white pullets. She could keep one cockerel for breeding and sell the other for a good price 'cause it was a pedigree Leghorn.

If you go farming you got to know all about breeding and all what you must do to get the best out of everything. Mother knew.

Mother and Ted about 1909

Father and His Work

He was born in 1859 in Dorset, I think at Piddletrenthide but I'm not sure, he never talked about himself. His mother, Elizabeth Spencer, was a servant with some titled people. She was very pretty and the son of the house went after her and then she had a baby – that was Father. She died soon after, but Mother told us we got our good looks and clear skin from Dad's mother. Well, then her employers — they were Father's grandparents when you come to think of it — found some people to bring him up and see he got "good training." They put him in a dairy and he learned how to separate milk, make butter and cheese.

When he was older he found work as a cowman and one day he had to take a herd to Winfrith. Mother was there helping her father with his cows. She was about twenty, and she took one look at Father, dark-haired, good-looking, and said to herself, "That's who I'm goin' to marry." They did marry in 1882, lived a few more years in Dorset and then moved to Wiltshire, first to Poulshot, then Roundway, near Devizes, on Lord Roundway's[2] estate.

My parents were at Roundway for seven years, then they had to move to Burbage. They were five years there and I was born at the end of that time, in 1899. I was only five months when we left so the first place I can remember Father working is Coombe Farm.

He was out on the Plain with his herd and two dogs seven days a week, in all weathers. He got no holidays, even Bank Holiday meant perhaps just half a day off. If there was a fête at Everleigh or a wedding or some'ing he might get off early but only after all the animals had been fed.

His day would start at six in the morning with feeding the calves in the skillins.[3] They were kept in three separate lots: first the little calves, they had to have special food, next came older calves and last came twelve-month old ones that would be gradually going out into the meadow by day. Hay was put in racks for they to go and feed. Then Dad had to grind up roots for them and put it in layers: chaff, mangels, crushed oats, swedes, crushed oats again and a layer of chaff on top. They had that twice a day.

Then about eight o'clock the big herd had to be taken on the hills with the two dogs – the cows would run all over the place if Dad never had his dogs with him. One of the dogs was called Carlo, I remember Dad brought him home as a puppy; he was lovely, a big dog, cream and black. The other one I remember was Benjamin, Benjy.

Dad had to stay all day with the cows — you've got no idea how carefully cattle were looked after in those days. You couldn't leave them because for instance the foxhounds might come or the soldiers, and then the cattle would be gone. They couldn't be fenced in because the land belonged to the government.

Those must have been long, lonely days for a man that liked company. He was lucky if a shepherd passed sometimes and stopped for a word. Once he come home and said he'd met one of the royal dukes! (Gloucester was it, or York). He was out with the hunt and gave Dad half a crown as they passed through the gate he was holding open.

At lunchtime in winter Dad lit a fire to keep warm while he ate what Mother'd packed up. Sometimes he spent the time carving little toys out of wood, perhaps a little boat for Ted to sail on the pond. Then there were the little animals he could trap.

Moles needed killing because they damaged the grass and then the cattle did suffer. So Father would put traps down one day and collect the dead moles the next; then skin them and stretch the skins on a board so they dried, rabbit skins too. And if the dogs caught a hare or a fox, he would get that skin too. They had to be taught to kill them without tearing the skin. Sometimes if the hunt was out the fox would go under the gorse. (A lot of the gorse on the Plain has gone now, but there used to be gorse and juniper bushes.) Well, if they were hunting and the fox got tired he would crouch in these bushes where they were thick. Sometimes Father would see a fox go there; he'd say nothing to the hunt, but when they'd gone he'd let his dogs go and kill it, carefully so as to keep the tail. The tail was what fur merchants did like — fox furs you see. The moleskins could be made into hats, waistcoats and jackets, and Dad did send all these skins to Collins, fur people in the East End of London.

At four o'clock he brought the herd back and the next job would be feeding and watering the calves again. At times when a cow was calving he stayed up all night looking after her, with a kettle on the boil to make a drench. That would help to clear everything away after the birth. Then the cow stayed in the shed for three days so he could keep a careful eye on her.

It was a hard, dreary life and Dad looked forward to getting away once a year to Salisbury Fair. It was a good thirty miles' walk and rough going. He did get up very early and Mother packed him up as much food as he could carry in a knapsack.

There'd be one lad with him and the dogs and they'd take the heifers to sell, those that wasn't good for breeding. They'd be away about a week, three days on the way because you can't drive cows too hard, and three days getting back. They had to drive them gently so they didn't get frightened and scatter, let them drift along, feeding as they went. At night they stopped, penned the cattle up and found somewhere to lie down themselves's best they could. They walked right through the Plain, travelling the old Roman road but not too near Bulford Camp, skirted round Salisbury and went on to Downton Fields where the Fair was.

When they got there they had to find the right pens for their cattle. Then it was off to the pub for a drink. You could get a piece of bread with it but Father never ate anything if he was on the drink. He and the boy had to find a barn or stable to sleep in because no-one would take drovers in. That's why they had to take their food with them, and when it was gone it was gone.

It might be pouring with rain but they'd still have to sleep rough and put up with it.

The next day he stayed with the cattle till they were all sold. If he couldn't sell them all, it would mean a slow journey home.

He always brought something home for Mother; once it was those two oil paintings and another time a lovely piece of velvet. (There's a photograph of her wearing that velvet in the front of her dress.) Then there'd usually be a big bag of humbugs for Ted and me. We did run down the field when we saw him coming, so glad he was back.

Dad was very different from Mother, light-hearted, a bit like me. He loved singing and he had a lovely voice. When he was young he used to play a violin on Bournemouth sands to get a few pennies. But after they married Mother put it on the fire because music usually went with drinking. Now, Mother was in charge of paying the bills so she always took Father's ten shillings' wages and any overtime he got; but when the money for the mole-skins did come from London that was his pocket money, so then he might have a drinking bout. Down the taproom of the Crown at Everleigh and a good old sing-song with the soldiers from Tidworth. My brother Ted used to worry a lot about Father drinking, but I loved to hear Dad coming home with the soldiers, all so happy: Just a song at twilight, Sweet Adeline, Alice, where art thou? In the Gloaming, — I can still hear those old songs.

The only time he went to Enford for his drink was at election time. Father always voted Liberal. "Tories," he'd say, "That's for the rich. Liberals is for the working man." Voting was at Enford and Polling Day was a special time so it was off to the Swan for a drink, and then perhaps a few more. It was all right because the pony would bring him home. He'd just turn it round, or if he was too tipsy for that, the other men would put him in the cart, put the pony right and home he'd go.

But for Mother there was always the worry of him losing his job, because it'd happened once when they were at Round-

way before I was born. It was one day when he had to go to
Calne to deliver eggs and butter to a factory. Instead of coming
home afterwards he went to the pub and stayed there so long
the pony and trap went home without him. Poor Mother had
to do his cows, Lord Roundway's bailiff found out, Father was
sacked and out of their cottage and away they had to go — to
Burbage as it turned out.

Sometimes on the Plain too Dad would get fed up, leave the
cows and go off. Once I remember he didn't come home at four
o'clock and Mother started worrying. She asked a shepherd
that was coming in and he said Father'd gone off. She had to
go nearly into Bulford rounding up the cows. So the next day
she went to the publican at Everleigh and said "Don't you dare
serve him again with a pint or I can have the law on you." In
those days you could say that to a publican if you had someone
like that in the family.

But if he did come home drunk, she knew how to deal with
him — shut him in the woodhouse with a bucket o' water.
They're always very thirsty after a bout, so he could drink
water from the bucket until his system was clear. This didn't
worry me because he kept on singing in the woodhouse so I
thought everything must be all right. He never argued with
Mother about shutting him in, always let her take charge.

Dad had a soft spot for all his girls. He cried when the three
little ones died of diphtheria and when Annie had her trouble.

He worked hard all his life. When he'd finished the farm
work there was his garden and jobs like sawing wood and
getting coal in for Mother – she never had to do nothing like
that. In the winter there was always making and mending to
do indoors; it might be the rag rugs or sorting out his dried
peas and beans ready for next year's planting. At eighty-two
he was still walking half a mile backwards and forwards to the
well most of Saturday morning getting water in two buckets
on a yoke to fill the copper for our baths.

One day, about 1942, he came in very tired and said,

"There you are, I've dug your garden. I sha'n't be doin' it
any more."

Father in old age

The next day he said, "I don't think I can get up today," and he died.

He had a wonderful funeral — children and grandchildren, with John, Jim and Teddy in their Army and Navy uniforms. He would've liked that.

A Pattern of Days, Weeks, Months and Years

Mother was a great one for routines. Our day began at six and ended with supper at eight and bed at nine. Then there were weekly routines.

Saturday was cleaning day and Ted and I had our share of the work — no playing about for us. I had to scrub the brick floor in the kitchen, the toilet at the back and the stairs. If you didn't scrub properly and let the water run you got lines down the stairs and then you had the whole lot to do again.

And don't talk to me about how lovely it is picking elderberries and elderflowers to make wine! I had to spend summer mornings picking bags and bags of them and it wasn't so lovely. Then on Saturday afternoons we were usually sent wooding. Out would come the little cart Father made for us to harness to Mother's big billy goat, a horrible beast that kept trying to knock you down. We had to take him to the woods and fill the cart ready for the winter.

I'm afraid I never did any of these jobs willingly. There was always that little feeling that I ought to have had a better life. I used to say to Ted, "If Mother'd let me be adopted I wouldn't be doing all this, I'd be doing ..." (I didn't quite know what). But I still think, old as I am, I was done out of a lot. Mother herself often said I wasn't meant for work and complained that I was different from my sisters. Yes, I was, because I wanted to do better than them. I didn't want a drab life, I wanted to do things, make things, read, find out about the world, learn how all sorts of things was made, learn about the past — history — and most of all I wanted to learn music and play the piano.

It was no use grumbling to Ted. He just got on with his job grinding up all the roots to feed the calves, so Father wouldn't have to do it on Sunday.

Then Saturday evening Father used to fill the copper and light it for out baths in the kitchen, in a tin bath in front of the stove. Dad always had his bath in the woodhouse because he would never dream of undressing in front of Mother. They were very strict about that sort of thing. I had my hair washed and plaited up tight, then we had to put our bits of toys away ready for Sunday.

Sundays, well Sunday morning Mr. Maton came to have a look round. He had a big black horse and we had to hold it while he did his round. Then if the afternoon was fine we had to walk the three miles to Enford for Sunday school. If it was wet, well then Mother read to us from some religious book she'd got from the vicar. On no account could we play on a Sunday. Sometimes I did long to be able to go out and have a good run!

In the afternoon Mother put on a clean white apron and made a fruit cake or perhaps some of her wonderful lardy cakes. If it was winter we stayed in after tea 'cause it would be getting dark, but in the summer it was back to Enford for Evensong. So if I don't know about religion now, who do?

Every fortnight in summer we went to Marlborough Saturday market — if Mother had a good pony for the trap. The best one she ever had was Tom, a black one Mr. Maton got from the army at Salisbury Fair. Tom lived about thirty years but once he died she got no more ponies. Most people had bikes by then and Mr. Maton thought Mother ought to be able to manage.

Once a month she did put on her best dress and go to Enford for the Mothers' Union, tea and talks from the vicar and his wife. All the mothers talked about how to manage with fuel, food and clothes for the family; perhaps they'd be shown how to cut out a shirt or a dress by the ladies of the village.

Then there was the Clothing Club. Mother did pay in two shillings a month and the Club would make the money up to so much. If she couldn't go to the Mothers' Union meeting the vicar would walk up and see her, have a few prayers and collect the two shillings.

At the end of these afternoons Father did go and get Mother in the trap. Ted and me had to lay the supper and keep the kettle boiling. She'd bring home some cake what was left from the tea. I can remember it all well, and feeling happy and cared for.

Then once a year Mother went, by carrier, to Devizes to spend what she'd saved through the Clothing Club. The carrier ran a smallholding in Upavon but when he drove to market he picked up people in Enford that wanted to go to Devizes. There was room for several down each side of his canvas-topped waggon. In Devizes Mother had to go to a certain shop that had an arrangement with the Clothing Club. They'd look at her list and say something like — well now, you can have a pair of shoes, and so many yards of calico. (That was to make our chemises and nightdresses. We never had like they have now — it was all calico. You couldn't buy a shirt, you had to make everything. Calico was a penny a yard and we had it for sheets, pillow cases and underclothes). They did count out every penny, and if what you wanted came to too much you wasn't able to have everything on the list. That was their rules and Mother was just as careful, she didn't want anything unless she paid for it; because if you did get into debt you went to prison, you'd lose your job and your home, they'd take your furniture and everything. Like Mother said, if you got into debt you'd never be able to pay back 'cause you didn't get any more money one week that the week before.

There was never any money for anything we didn't really need.

Up at Everleigh Manor, the big house, they did have parties and people did come from London on in big carriages and all that. We didn't see anything of them, but when there was a shoot it was different. On the Downs they did have big shoots; sometimes it would be hares and sometimes partridges (not pheasants, pheasants used to be the other side of Everleigh in the woods.)

There was a room at the side of our cottage where the ladies and gentlemen from the shoot came to eat. At the end of summer, someone would come and tell Father he must whitewash it all out ready for the autumn shoots. Mother must have everything ready on the day, tables laid and a roaring fire. Two men used to come in white coats, the butler and — the chef, was it? Anyway, Mother used to say to the butler, "Yes, Sir," and all *very important*. On the day of the shoot the horse would come with the food and everything, and it was thought a very big day. We children had to be kept indoors, we wasn't supposed to see anything of it or be about. Mother used to say, "You mustn't come out 'cause the ladies are here." But we did peep round the corner when they did come in.

They did get all the stray men that had no work to be beaters, and they did have sandwiches outside the cottage.

We looked forward to this day 'cause when all the people and all the white coats had gone there was a feast left over for us, lots of delicious things. Mother was paid, I think a shilling a week to keep the room clean and she was always keen to get these little extras.

"I'm not going to be bothered with that. You can take it home."

Just what Mother wanted to hear from Mr. Maton whenever he had a litter of pigs and there was what they call a runt. She'd take it home, and 'course you got to feed them with warm milk and roll it in a warm blanket or it would die. Having the goats, you see, she had milk for the little pig. Then as it got bigger it could have a mixture of mangels, swedes, potatoes and the boiled grain Mother got from Netheravon Brewery. When it had grown to nine score it had to be killed. It was a real big "do", the pig being killed. The stool and everything that was used had to be thoroughly scrubbed and clean. When the man came to do it we were put to bed, we wasn't never allowed to see that. And the pig did squeal! But we never thought nothing about having a pig killed — it was our food for the winter.

Then the bench in the woodhouse would be scrubbed and the pig hung there till the blood had drained out, for two weeks. It was salted with an exact amount of salt petre and cut up. Father would do the sides of bacon. We had the hams and the trotters and Mother made brawn with the head. You got lovely liver and all that and she would get bowls of pure lard. Some of the fat meat you frizzled down and made lovely scrap pies with apples in and raisins in. You can't make them now 'cause butchers don't keep scraps — no-one would buy them.

We killed a pig about twice a year and shared it with neighbours — Mrs. Maggs and Mrs. Wiltshire were two I remember. Then they shared theirs with us when they killed it. Mother often sent lard to my sister Kate in Southampton. It was taken down in the trap to Collingbourne Ducis Station and put on the train.

Father kept half the vegetable garden specially to grow pig-food and Mother did all the looking after the little pig — we wasn't interested in that. I liked animals but they were either for work or food. We never had much chance to make pets of them.

Sisters

They were all so much older than me. Jane was the next one up and even she was eight years older, but she and Maggie were still at home when I was born. I saw the others when they came for holidays but that wasn't very often, and it was difficult for them to come after they married because mostly they had no means of getting about. And they couldn't write well enough to send letters. So I don't know much about what they did or what they were like as children.

They'd all gone into service by the time I was six. Parents couldn't afford to keep girls at home so when they got to a certain age they had to go to the only job they knew. There was never any question of anything else, and they all took it for granted, the rough, hard life and everything — all except me because I always wanted to do something better.

First was Bessie; she was born in 1878, four years before Mother married. We never heard who her father was. Mother never talked about it, but I s'pose it was why Bessie stayed with Mother's parents in Winfrith and they brought her up. P'raps that's why Mother was so worried about all of us girls and afraid of us getting into trouble. I didn't know for years that Bessie was only a half sister until Edie said one day, "I'm the eldest really."

Bessie was big and dark and handsome like Mother and the only one of us that didn't go into service. She went to London when she was fourteen and worked, Mother said, in a confectioner's. All I can remember of Bessie's London days is her coming home in beautiful clothes. We used to meet her at the station and I can see her now in this great big hat with flowers piled on top of it. It was so wide she had to turn sideways to get out of the carriage.

Poor Bessie didn't want a lot of children, so she didn't marry until she was thirty-two, hoping that would avoid it. Then she married Harry Hawkins and had six, the last when she was forty-two. She was strong, like most of us and lived to a hundred and two!

Edith and Kate were rather alike, I think, tallish and dark-haired. Edie married a carter, John Chandler, and Kate married a docker in Southampton ... I know he drank heavy and I believe she died when she was thirty-five of heart trouble.

Between Edie and Kate came Annie. She was small and thin, but wiry. Her first job was feeding the deer in Savernake Forest, then when she was thirteen she went into service in Marlborough.

One day in 1899 — I was only a baby but Jane told me later — they heard Annie was being sent home. There was a terrible to do, but Jane and Maggie didn't know what it was about, no-one would tell them but Annie had committed a dreadful sin. She came home and at last they found out that she was like to have a baby. But how had it happened?

Father, always so fond of his girls, was crying over it, but the first thing Mother did was to give Annie a good whipping and the next day she took her in the trap to Pewsey Workhouse. It sounds hard, but then if daughters misbehaved it was goodbye to the cottage and Father's job. Farmers was always turning people out for that sort of thing. All Maggie and Jane were told was that if it happened to them they'd go to the same place.

The trouble came, it seemed, from not keeping away from men. I later picked up this warning too and all my single days it was in my mind: Never be alone with a man. I didn't know why but I grew up with this fear.

Years later Annie told me how it was this man did do the wood and coal and clean the boots at the house where she worked. Same as she said, he pushed her over and she wasn't strong enough to fight him. Fourteen year olds then weren't as strong as they are today.

"You don't know what I went through." She was very bitter, she never came back home and I don't think she ever forgave Mother.

She must've been miserable slaving away at the workhouse and having to eat that horrible skilly.[4] She had the baby and then the workhouse found her a job working for three old ladies at Weston-super-Mare. They said she could keep her baby but he must be kep' upstairs and no-one must ever see him.

Later on Annie married a widower and had, I think, eight more children. But they wouldn't take any notice of Albert, this first son, because of how he came to be born. That sort of thing was terrible looked down on. But after I was married we used to go and see them sometimes and my husband always chatted to Albert and took him out to the pub, never treated him different. That meant a lot to Annie.

There were more terrible times in store for her and yet somehow she lived to ninety-three.

Nell, now she was the prettiest of us girls; I think she got her lovely curls from Dad's mother. She went to work for Mr.

Gauntlett's family, a rich farmer in Collingbourne. The Gauntletts had three grown-up daughters that never married and Nell waited on them all. Later she married the farm foreman, Jack Smith, and the Gauntletts paid for the wedding. Mother and Dad were invited, and Mother told us later about Nell's mauve wedding dress. Jane stayed home with me and I remember she made us a potato pie.

Maggie, her looks were different again; dark eyes but a pale complexion. Different in her ideas too, she always had everything worked out. She was always changing jobs, and oh, she was a great worry to Mother. She would leave a job, not write home — they never knew what she was doing. At last Mother found her a job in Bradford-on-Avon in a public school kitchen. There was a young Swiss there, Martin, had come over to learn to be a sweetcook — learn how to make cakes and decorate them, everything in that line.

Martin couldn't speak a word of English. After he'd learned his trade at Bradford he had to move on, so he got a job in an hotel in Yorkshire. The next thing Mother heard was that Maggie'd gone with him. She was in a great state about that for some time because Maggie didn't write and Mother was afraid about what might be going on.

When she heard they'd got married she stopped worrying. This was a little while before the Great War. Then they left Yorkshire and came to London, took a house in Brixton, let the top two flats and lived on the ground floor. They stayed there all through the war and adopted two girls, Heidi and Betty. (Maggie did have a baby of her own but she lost it.)

While they were in London, Maggie got talking to Mother during one of her visits home, said I needed training and should get this by going to help her look after Heidi and Betty. I hadn't gone into service by then, so Mother agreed and I was put on the train to go to Maggie's for a spell. I didn't get on well — she was always finding fault and telling tales to Mother.

Mother always liked for Maggie and Martin to come down to Wiltshire because they did bring things like haddocks, and cakes he'd made. They were visiting us one day after the war when some papers came saying Martin had to leave the hotel he worked at. He'd never been naturalised and now they were moving foreign workers out to make jobs for our ex-servicemen. So Martin went back to Switzerland and Maggie and the girls went later. They settled down there, and stayed for several years.

Maggie and her daughters visiting Martin in hospital, 1920s

Then Martin got a job in Denmark, so they moved there. One day our Prince of Wales happened to be staying in the hotel where Martin was working, so Martin made a cake with the Prince o' Wales feathers decorating it. Out came the Prince to shake hands because, he said, he'd never seen the feathers in sugar before!

Martin had a long bicycle ride home every night into the country where they lived. One night, going out from the hot kitchen, he caught a chill and died of it. I don't know how Maggie felt about his death. We didn't get on and I never saw her again after she married so I didn't think much about it. Things just happened.

She stayed in Denmark until just before the Second World War, then she and the girls came back. Maggie arranged jobs in Wiltshire for the girls, and after all that travelling, Heidi and Betty ended up there with Wiltshire husbands. Maggie went off to Yorkshire again to do a housekeeper's job, met a widowed greengrocer and married him. That was the last I heard about her.

Jane I got on better with. She and Nell and I all had a look of Father about us, except that we had very fair hair and his was dark. Jane was not quite fourteen when her time came to leave us. Out of the blue one day Mother said, "Kate says you can have a place with her at Eastleigh." So we had to get poor Jane ready. Mother found the money for her uniform — parents always had to — and off she went into service near Southampton for the next five years.

In 1910, when she was nineteen, Jane came home to marry George Ferris, a shepherd working on the same farm as Father. George had fought in the Boer War and was much older than Jane, but very good-looking. She married on Christmas Eve and had the loveliest wedding dress: A high neck, with tucks in the bodice and sleeves, lace trimming and an embroidered skirt, all in cream, and a cream hat with orange blossom. I suppose she loved George but I don't know — we never talked about loving.

We kept in touch and I went to help with her first baby

Jane with her daughters Doris and Maud 1917

when I was thirteen. She had eight more but her favourite was always Jim. He went in the Marines in the Second War — killed on D-Day.

The three little girls that died before I was born were Amy, Fanny and Ethel. When they went down with diphtheria, Lady Savernake used to visit and try to help Mother. I was told that Fanny, the baby, was dark and always had a frightened look. Mother complained that she was frightened by a black man when she was expecting her. Amy, Mother said, was lovely, always wanted to be dressed in white, and when they gave her a little go-cart to play with she used to fill it up with toys and say she was going to visit the angels. She was four when she died. Perhaps it was Amy's looks that gave Lady Savernake the idea of adopting one of us.

After losing these three, Mother had twins in 1899. One, a boy, was born dead, the other one was me!

Ted

Mother was forty-two when my brother was born and she did have a very bad time. He was a blue baby — the nurse said he was all blue and they had to give him a little brandy in milk every day before his feeds. I don't remember any doctor seeing him about his heart, but then no-one ever though of the doctor unless you were dying. All I know is Mother said he had a very delicate heart. But he still walked the three miles to school every day and worked hard all his life. But when he died at seventy-three it was because his heart gave way, suddenly.

We didn't treat Ted any different because he was a boy — well, perhaps Mother did. I knew him better than my sisters because we two grew up together after they'd all gone away. When we were little our favourite game was getting married and making a house. I'd dress up as a bride in an old long white dress out of one of Mother's boxes; then we'd make a house in the gorse bushes, with things like flower pots and cardboard boxes for furniture.

Mother taught us always to share things; he'd have half my apple, he'd give me half his chocolate. She didn't say anything about sharing our thoughts and troubles but we often did.

Ted was a worrier and so often afraid of Mother getting angry ... always saying "You mustn't, Win," like when I wanted to buy sweets with the penny I was supposed to put in the Post Office; and when we did steal the eggs from under the hens, and when I made him run off with me to Larkhill to see one of the first aeroplanes. Oh, and he did so worry about Father's drinking and singing, and I didn't worry a bit — I liked to see Father happy and jolly. All his life Ted never went into pubs.

He left school at thirteen instead of fourteen, but first he had to take an exam to see if he'd learnt enough to leave and go on the land. This was when there was such a need for men in the army that they were releasing everyone from the land and putting boys there to replace them. Ted passed the exam and

Ted, aged about thirteen

that was the end of his schooling.

He worked on Maton's Farm, same as Father; mostly agricultural work — sowing, harvesting, thrashing — but sometimes helping with sheep and cattle. He didn't like farming but he had to do it, like me having to go off to service, no ifs or buts.

He tried to get out of it though. One day when he was a bit older he went up to the village and a lad from there, just back from Swindon, told Ted they wanted men at the railway works. Ted had always wanted to drive an engine and they thought they'd both go along and see if they could get taken on. When Ted told me I thought it would be wonderful for him. He loved engines, even those big ploughing engines he did drive sometimes.

But when Mother heard about it there was a big fuss. OH DEAR — HOW DREADFUL! . And where would he live??? I told her I had to leave home and get on with it, so why not Ted? "Oh," she said, "You *would* think different." Daughters could leave home but not sons — she always wanted sons.

She wouldn't let him go. Spoilt his life, I always thought. She did that sort o' thing. Another time, his friend in the Guards said why didn't Ted join with him — he was tall

Mr. Maton's chauffeur, instructing school leavers,
one is possibly Ted

enough. "Try it, my lad, and I'll break you legs," said Mother. Father never interfered, she ran the whole show.

When Ted was seventeen he did volunteer for the army, in spite of her. They called him for a medical but no, he wasn't fit enough. Poor Ted.

Child Bearing

In families like ours they never did nothing not to have children. If a baby was coming, well, a baby was coming – you just got on with it. (It was different with the better-off people.) When my mother did keep on having children and people said about it she used to say, you see, The Lord will provide. There was no question of anything else. But when I was in service in Newbury there was a lady doctor[5], she wrote a book about it. There was a lot about her in the papers and they said that she was wicked and all sorts of things and she was working with the devil.

When I got married and I never had a child for eight years they all said I knew something not to have children but I didn't. Now my sister Nell, she had a baby, then a miss then five more children. She said to me once "I'd have had twenty children altogether, counting all the misses." Nell wasn't strong enough, her children came too close together, and that's why they were all delicate. They all died early from heart attacks and before their mother.

Like my sister Jane. Well, Jane had Maud and Doris, Thora, Joyce and Jim; then she had twin boys and had a very bad time with them. She was so ill the doctor told her husband George: It's no good, you mustn't have any more children if you want to keep your wife. After that she had John, but then she went five years. Then she had Desmond, but with Dessy she had to go down in the village and be taken great care of, the nurse visit her every day and some special treatment. Then she never had no more. The doctor may have given her something after she had John so that she went five years, I don't know.

All Hands!

Mr. Maton was a very wealthy farmer. The Army bought up everything from him — grain, bull calves, mutton to feed the troops and wool for their greatcoats. All this trade meant his labourers had to turn their hands to anything. Dad often had to help with the sheep, Mother and other women were needed at harvest and haymaking, and whenever Ted and I were on holiday from school there was sure to be work for us.

The worst job was the stone picking we had to do in the winter, starting at seven in the morning. You had to fill a bucket and so many buckets made a heap. You smoothed the heap out to make a square yard for the foreman to measure and it had to be certain depth, about one foot I think. Sixpence was paid for each square yard and the stones were used to repair the road leading to the farm. All farmers had to see these by-roads were kept up. I remember the first time I was taken to the stony field and given a bucket. My hands hurt in the bitter wind and I tucked them under my arms, until Mother gave me a clip and said "Get on with it."

Later in the year there was sheep dipping and shearing. At shearing time Ted and I had to get up at four in the morning to help with the rounding up. We rode little ponies for this, Welsh ponies rescued from the pits — rounding up sheep was supposed to be a rest for them. Of course Dad used his dogs too for this job.

There would be four shearers working all day. I watched them do it and I know how to shear. Sit the sheep with its back to you, on its bottom; you cut the top round its head, then you go round the neck, then turn it over on its side and cut half the back, turn it on the other side and cut that. Father didn't shear, but he did pack all this. Mother was there, rolling up the big fleeces, then a boy used to wind out a long cord and tie them up. And every pack had to have the name of the flock and the type of sheep because you see there was Hampshire Downs, Large White, Large and small Black (that was white and black-faced sheep); Every lot was a different wool and had to be put in a different bag and Father did pack it all.

Then at the right season sheep must be dipped, to keep the ticks and all that out. They'll get fleas and maggots and lose their wool if they're not dipped. Flocks from farms all over the Plain were brought along, each with their own shepherd. George Ferris, the man that married my sister Jane, was our shepherd.

Dipping was a big "do", they'd have a week at it. On dipping day the cows had to stay at the farm because Father had to help with the sheep. You'd have one man pushing them into the dipping pit and others poking them down into the water with long rods. The dipping water was very poisonous and no-one went near the pit except these workers, and they wore special overalls.

One very hot dipping day Benjy the dog came home and Mother could see he was ill. He lay down and died and she said he must've been drinking the poison water. Dad was very upset when he saw him 'cause he was always kind to his

Sheep dipping at Enford about 1902

animals, looked after them, always saw they were fed before he had his own dinner, that kind of thing. And of course Benjy was valuable to him, good at his job and perfectly trained.

At hay-making time Mother and the other women were in the hayfield by six in the morning. Their job was to turn the hay over with long forks — this was in the days before they had machines to do that. Later, when it was dry, they'd make heaps — what they called "pook it up",[6] a word they had for it. Then a horse would bring along a waggon to be loaded. Father was the pitcher, tossing the haycocks into the cart. Then there was the loader, his job was to spread the hay evenly so it balanced in the waggon. When all was loaded the waggon was taken to the rickyard and there four men made the rick. Two at the bottom did put the hay in the elevator and it did go up to the two men at the top — six men altogether (with pitcher and loader) whereas today they never have but one man. While they were doing this, Mother and the others were in another field getting more hay ready for the waggon.

Harvest was the one time children were expected to stay away from school to help. We got sixpence a week for our work. Reaping and binding was done by machines drawn by horses, but women's hands were needed for the stooking. One of my jobs was to make a pit, light a fire and brew tea for four of them — Mother, Mrs. Maggs, Mrs. Spreadbury and one other name I can't remember. Once they shouted at me because the stubble had caught fire. I had to run and tell the men, they rushed to the pump, soaked some sacks and managed to put the fire out before it spread.

Later it would be time to make the ricks. The big waggon must be drawn along the rows of stooks, someone leading the horse. One year the men came to our cottage early and said they wanted Ted to do this. Mother was upset — he was only five — but they said, "We must 'ave 'im, we're short-handed," and that was that. When the waggon was full, a second horse was harnessed in front of the first with chains to help pull the heavy load to the rickyard. When they'd done, the tired horses could be taken to have a plash in the pond.

In the autumn the ricks were taken apart for the thrashing by machine. One of the women fed the sheaves into the machine and the grain did come down and fill the bag at the bottom. When it was all done the man in charge used to let the machine go on running to clear out the inside. He usually gave Mother a bag of these kevins[7] for her hens to scratch and peck about in. Working people helped each other like that.

When there was ploughing to do Mr. Maton put his carters on to it. But if a field had been down to grass it would be too tough for the horse plough so they used these ploughing engines, one each side of the field with a belt between the two and the plough in the middle. We couldn't help with that, but I often wished I could have a go.

I felt like that about most things. I even wanted to see how a dead horse was skinned. Ted kept well away from that but I didn't see anything to get upset about. I knew it had to be done and it was something else I could learn by watching, like the sheep shearing.

All the old carthorses, carriage horses and pit ponies that were past working were put out to grass together. Dad kept an eye on them for Mr. Maton and if he saw one that couldn't get up he sent for the knackermen. I was there one day when they came, two short fat men, to look at one old horse. I knew what they would say:

"Well, Jim, he've had his day, he'll never get up again."

Straight away the three of them started digging a hole. They shovelled lime into it. One of them shot the horse cleanly in the head, gone in a flash. Then a minute or two's rest and a smoke before starting on the skinning, not too long because it had to be done while the body was warm. They cut from the neck right down the front and tore off the skin. All the insides, bar the liver and heart, was burned in the lime pit. They'd sent for the Tidworth houndsman and he came and cut up the rest of the meat and took it, and the liver and heart, to feed his hounds. The skin went to the tannery.

Dad didn't mind me watching a horse killing, but seeing the Big Horse was another matter. "Don't you let those children out today," he told Mother. "The Big Horse is coming from Everleigh." For once I was too scared to disobey. Something in Dad's voice put fear of the Big Horse into me. It was like my fear of men. The Big Horse was coming because a mare was in season.

Postmen, Police and Poachers

About the only callers we had at Coombe Bake were the baker — he did bring groceries as well as bread — and of course the postman. His visit was important because that was the way we heard news of what did go on down in the village, and other news about the rest of the world too. I remember him telling us about the sinking of the Titanic in 1912 and how everyone was talking about it because the ship was supposed to be unsinkable.

A good postman was very important to us out there but a lazy one would just give letters to anyone who happened to be coming up our way or just leave them till he felt like coming up in the next day or so. After I'd married and we were living at Coombe Bake for a while my husband lost the chance of a good job because the postman never bothered to deliver a letter on time.

One postman's story was about a murder at Netheravon. A man, he said, had murdered his six children and laid them all out in a row on a bank, the eldest first and so on. The saying goes that if a murder happens at midnight and you go where it happened, at midnight, you're sure to see something of it. People say they've gone there, to Netheravon, not thinking about the murder at all but at the very time it happened and there they see the children — all white — laid out on the bank in the moonlight.

One day the postman told Mother there was to be a hanging. A police sergeant had been shot. What happened was the Enford constable had asked the sergeant at Netheravon to recommend him for promotion. The constable was supposed to report for work at a certain gate at ten p.m., but when he heard that the sergeant wouldn't recommend him, he'd gone at ten p.m. and shot the sergeant. (I was listening while the postman was telling Mother this. No, I wasn't frightened, never frightened, 'cept of cows, never frightened to go anywhere on my own, or the dark, and if someone was to attack me now, I'd attack him, kick his legs — he would have a shock!)

Poachers were all around; they would creep about in the gorse dodging the keepers, catching hares and pheasants and partridges, all that kind of thing, and they would know how to send the skins off to London to be sold. We always had to have good dogs because if you didn't watch out, poachers might take a calf or anything. But Mother never turned anyone from the door, poachers or anyone. If one of them asked for a drink, she never refused because, she said, what they did was their business; and she'd fill their cans with tea any time.

Well, one day the police came. (Ted and I went off and hid because we'd often been told they'd get us if we were naughty.) It seemed they'd been after a certain poacher for years and now they'd found someone dead on the hills and they suspected him of the murder. They asked Mother if he'd been to our cottage. She said yes, he come one pouring wet day, wet through. The police asked if they could look round and they went everywhere — barns, stables and then the woodhouse. In there Mother kept Father's old clothes, hung up clean to use for patching. But this time they found the poacher's wet clothes hung up there instead. So I suppose he must have went in the woodhouse, p'raps in the night, changed into Father's things and gone off ... I never found out whether he did do the murder.

Soldiers and Gypsies

The military were very much part of our lives on the Plain. They weren't restricted, could go anywhere they liked and this was a real worry to anyone looking after animals. They'd come galloping down among them — away go the sheep, away go the cows, and you'd have to hunt all over for them. Sometimes there'd be real big mock battles with smoke, barbed wire and guns firing. The red flag did go up and then it was your look-out if you got in the way. And they never compensated a farmer if a cow or a sheep got destroyed.

Still I always liked soldiers, it would've been dull without them. Every morning I listened for the six o'clock bugle and I miss that even now.

At night the Redcaps, the military police from Tidworth would come and round up any soldiers that were out of bounds. They sometimes put Everleigh out of bounds, you see, especially after any trouble at the Crown. The taproom there was always full of soldiers in the evening and if one had a drink too many he might get into an argument; then others would join in and end up with a good old fight — especially if any of the Black Watch from Perham Down were there as well as Tidworth men. Then it would be England against Scotland and what a set-to!

My mother would never let us go near any soldiers (remember Aunt Helen). Oh no! But I liked to see them marching around. And when I grew up and went into service in Newbury and met a lot of civilians, my sisters were always asking why I didn't have a "nice young man". And I'd say, "Oh no, I don't want no sissy boys." I wanted a soldier, because I thought they were MEN, not like those white-handed valets and footmen I met in service.

At one time I could tell you all the different regiments on the Plain, kilts and all. I can't tell why, but military bands have always given me a thrill. Even today when I see soldiers marching on TV I think to myself if I'd been the boy instead of

Ted I'd've made a good soldier. I could've done "left right" and I could tramp and I could obey — I could do it all!

Something else we saw a lot of on the Plain was gypsies, with their horses and carts, pots and pans and clothes pegs. Sometimes we saw them washing their babies in the troughs that were filled for the cattle — with cold water!

At night you could see their fires, but not if the Redcaps was about. They were always after the gypsies because they poached. They wasn't supposed to be on military ground but they camped in the woods, and those woods and the strip of ground in front of them, that was No-Man's Land — the military couldn't touch them there. But if they spotted gypsies outside the woods they'd have them.

Now, between Everleigh and Coombe Bake there's a huge big dip. In the bottom is a well and when there's a lot o' rain that fills up. But the gypsies knew when it would go dry and then they'd get down in that dip at night when the military couldn't see them. They'd set up a big net and then they did get their dogs to drive partridges, hares — everything — into that net. They knew where to sell what they caught all right, and if they could get a fox in that net — well, they knew what to do with *that* too! A foxtail meant a lot o' money and after all, they had to earn a living, same as we did.

They were real gypsies in those days and Mother warned us never to cross a gypsy or turn one away from the door. I've always remembered that, and many years later a gypsy brought me luck when my husband and I were in deep money trouble.

School

I started school at Everleigh when I was seven. It was a three-mile walk, and if it was raining, well you just got wet, and you stayed wet as far as the teachers were concerned.

There were two of them, the two Miss Browses, quite old ladies. They lived in the schoolhouse. I think they must have been highly qualified because when we used to have inspectors come they wore black gowns. Whether they were Oxford or not I'm not sure but I heard they'd come to Everleigh because they'd had some sort of illness. When they had their caps and gowns on they were specially strict and we knew someone important would be visiting — like on Fridays it was the clergy.

I didn't get on very well there and never got a good report and yet I always wanted to learn things. I was keen to play the piano and I used to peep at the music on the stand and try to work out the notes (I could read piano notes before I knew my letters.) I did this when we had singing lessons with doh, ray and me. I can pick out tunes now but I always wanted to learn to play properly. Then I wanted to learn dressmaking but we never got further than practising stitches on a bit of cloth, never made a whole garment.

I loved reading and still do. Sometimes someone at school would lend me books but Mother wouldn't let me read till I'd finished some mending, washing up or other job at home.

There were six Standards and you had to work hard in the upper ones. I remember geography lessons in Standard Five. Each of us had to be an English county and once I was Buckinghamshire. I wore a card with "Bucks" written on it and I had to learn all about that county, how it was all farming, not industrial. Whoever was "Durham" had to learn about coal mining. They gave you a book to read it up one week and then the next week you had to write about it. We did compositions the same way, hearing about something one week, writing about it the next. One week in 1910 it was the Corona-

tion, how King George was King Edward's second son, all
about what the King and Queen had to do, why they were
there. Another week it was Captain Scott's expedition[8]; how
they set out with the dogs and everything, where they went
and how some of them died in the tent.

I never could remember things I had to recite, kept saying
it over and over to myself but when I had to stand up and say
it I couldn't. History was about battles, like Hastings and Wa-
terloo. Arithmetic was all put on the blackboard. I wasn't bad
at long division but there was some kind of long subtraction
I couldn't manage. It was all very stiff and starchy and you
wasn't allowed to ask questions.

In the top Standard they taught how to write a letter if you
was going for a job, with the name at the top and Dear Sir or
Dear Madam.

We wasn't allowed to mix with the boys; girls had to play
in one half of the playground and the boys in the other half —
it was divided with a chalk line; and the girls hung up their
coats in one lobby and the boys in another. But we must have
got together sometimes, now I come to think of it — I can
clearly remember Farmer Strong's boy from Lower Farm
grabbed me once and gave me a big kiss! I liked that.

Some of the children were treated as special. There were the
butler's children from Everleigh Manor (his name was Dancy)
and the keeper's, they lived in the forest. All these children of
Everleigh Manor workers and two or three that belonged to
the gardener at the vicarage, they sat in special places and had
special lessons. They did go home for lunch but we had to
bring ours — sandwiches and a bottle of tea — and eat it in the
schoolroom. They always kept these children separate and
that's what made me feel, always had the feeling, that why
should we not be taught the same. That was the start of my
noticing things that were unfair in life.[9]

Ted and me never had the cane. Oh, I remember two that
did, a boy and girl that did come from Lower Everleigh, used
to walk up. Oliver Ayres — he was killed in the war — and
what was the girl's name? Nell Salisbury! Oliver was a big lad

... Ted was very fond of him I remember. They were always late and one day someone told Miss Browse that they did go over the wall into Everleigh Manor gardens, that was why they were late. I can see it all today: she went and got her cane, they were brought in from over the wall and she said, Right! Now they're going to be severely punished because they've been doing things they shouldn't've been doing. (They were getting on, Oliver and Nell, a bit older than me.) And she said they'd got to bend over a chair and be thrashed in front of the school. She gave them three stripes each, and every time I felt it across my bottom.

Treats and Joys, Given and Stolen

The Christmasses I can remember at Coombe Bake there were four of us children — Maggie, Jane, Ted and me. Father made us little toys out of wood for presents — boats and dolls and things. He or Mother did paint them with the dyes she made from elderberries, beetroot, blackberries and onions, and she dressed the dolls.

We decorated with holly from the woods and of course Mother made puddings. A chicken and a pig would be killed for dinner ... Carol singers used to come up from the village with the clergyman ... On Boxing Day there would be fun. People came, one lot from Everleigh and another lot from Enford and they met in the middle at Coombe Bake and drank Mother's home-made wines and beer. There was dancing and playing on mouth organs, tambourines and bones — little bunches of bones they'd cleaned and tied together and they did rattle and click them ... and Father did sing and sing, and *not* have to be shut in the woodhouse!

Then there was always a party at Everleigh Manor for everyone. Mother did take us and we each had a little present and an orange and an apple. (The same did happen for Christmas at Burbage, and at Roundway when my sisters were younger every child would be given a beautiful pelisse

— a sort of cloak. It's all so different today but years ago the people in the big houses used to take an interest and visit the people. That's all finished now.)

Coronation Day 1910, and we were up early to get everything done, animals all fed. I was excited because I was going to wear my new hat, dress and button boots — I never had button boots ever before! The dress was white with pink spots, the hat was white and it had white flowers with yellow centres. Father was very happy, he had the day off ... Such lots of people ... all kinds of games. Mother won the egg and spoon race ... Father sang with the other men ... Soldiers all in red uniforms with their horses.

In the big meadow the other side of Everleigh Manor there was a big spread, all put out on tables with white cloths on ... the grown-ups one side and us the other ... they had their beer and everything and we had lemonade, and I believe, I'm not sure, but I think there was a cow roast. I never saw it — I didn't like to go near 'cause I thought the cow was alive! It was all served from a big tent.

We all ate a lot and then we had to line up to get our Coronation mugs from the Lady at Everleigh Manor ... a lovely day.

A fine Saturday in Summer meant a shopping trip to Marlborough, as long as Mother had a good pony. Ted and I must be up at six because it was twenty miles and you mustn't drive the pony too hard. We put on our best clothes 'cause we were going into town. On the way we stopped at a roadman's cottage just before Savernake Forest. Mother knew his wife and we always stopped there to give the pony a rest. Off again and after a while Marlborough came in sight. In the main street, a little ways in, was a public house where we could leave the trap and the pony would be given a good feed. Mother went round looking for bargains in the market — like a box of herrings for a shilling — and meeting people she'd known in Burbage and Collingbourne; people came on trains from all the villages around for market day. After the shopping we had a penny each to buy a bottle of lemonade and a Chelsea bun.

We didn't eat them straight away but on the way home we'd stop again — this time in the forest itself — for the tired pony. Then we had our lemonade and buns and I've never, never tasted such Chelsea buns as those!

Marlborough High Street with carts, 1901

All through the summer there were Army manoeuvres on the Plain. The Territorials and the OTC's from the public schools joined in this with the regulars. One year, it would be about 1907 when I was eight, we heard that King Edward was paying a visit at the end of manoeuvres to inspect them all. This was too exciting to miss and Mother took Ted and me to watch.

In a field about halfway between Everleigh and Netheravon there was a big tree — it's cut down now — and under it they made a platform for the King and important military men. A crowd of local people collected in the field opposite to

61

watch the troops march down the road in front of the King. As we waited there I thought how the soldiers would have been polishing their buttons and boots until everything shone, and seeing that every bit of their uniform was just right, caps dead straight, rifles in the right position.

We couldn't see the King very well, but we heard a band getting nearer and then the parade came past, cavalry first, then the artillery and then the foot soldiers and their bands, all in full dress uniform. I knew the Household Cavalry with their black horses, dead black they were, bred in Ireland, all beautiful and shining. Then the Lancers, their horses were all brown; and so many bands booming, clashing and piping; regiment after regiment — Scots, Welsh, Guards — trooping past so smart and lively and never-ending it seemed.

In the field where we were there was a row of balloons held down by ropes. They used these on manoeuvres to find out exactly where all the troops were, just as they would do in war. (This was in the days before they used aeroplanes for that.) Suddenly the soldier in charge asked Ted and me if we'd like to go up with a balloon. Of course we would! Up we did go and there was all the Plain below — farmhouses, fields and military buildings — for us to look down on. I felt grand and wondered what it would be like to fly.

I was going to see that aeroplane, I'd made up my mind. It'd been talked about all round the farms because it'd been made near us — at Upavon. It was one of the first to be made with a metal frame — before that they were wood. This one was going to fly from Upavon to Larkhill.

Coombe Bake and Enford were in the middle, between Upavon and Larkhill. We'd seen the plane go up like a big black bird and I worked out that if we ran to Larkhill we could see it there before they put it away. I made Ted come with me, running most of the eight miles, Ted worrying as usual about the trouble we would get into, but I wanted to see that plane. When we got there, there was a lot of people — I don't know whether the King was there, but Army people. This was at the time of the very beginning of the planes, there wasn't an Air Force but the fliers were part of the Army and they wore khaki suits.[10]

Well, we knew we musn't get in anyone's way, but we managed to get a good look. I felt I wanted to go up in that machine, like I'd gone in the balloon. (I was still wanting to fly after I was grown up, and at last when I was in my fifties I did fly — to Hong Kong to see my daughter.)

We were away all day and Mother didn't know where we were .... Yes, I got into trouble as usual. She smacked me hard, but it didn't matter. I'd had a lovely day.

Upavon Aerodrome, about 1913

I would've had more thrashings if Mother had realised some of the things I got up to. On Saturday mornings Ted and I were outside and I'd wait for the hens to start cackling. Then I'd tell Ted to creep in and get their eggs ... while I calmly asked Mother for some bread and butter. Then we went behind the pig sty, made a fire and boiled up the eggs in a cocoa tin and had a good feast. Poor Mother never did find out why she never had any eggs on Saturdays!

Then there was this lovely beer Mother did brew that she passed round to all the neighbours. She poured it in a big tub and when it was the right temperature she would put in the barm.[11] She kept it in the empty cottage next door. So, when she wasn't looking, in we would go, draw some off and put in a jar. Then Mother's beer would be spoiled because it'd been touched and the barm had sunk. She'd come out muttering, "The beer's spoilt again, the barm's gone down ..."

I enjoyed my jar, and then went to sleep under a bush ... I don't know what Ted did ...

If I heard that a lot of men were staying at the Crown Inn[12], I guessed they were there for the hare coursing. That meant

Crown Hotel, Everleigh

excitement, and as usual I wanted to join in. The coursing might take place in a field of stubble, with the hares being beaten out into it. They'd set two dogs after each hare, one on each side as it ran. One dog would give the hare a nip, and as it turned to run the other way the second dog would have it. The men laid bets and it was the dog that made the hare turn that was the winner. Yes, I'm afraid I did put a penny on if I had one. If I won anything, the beaters complained, said I should be at school and all that, but I usually got my money. Someone might tell Mother though, and then there'd be trouble, hands thrown in the air and "What on earth will that child do next?"

Getting Lost

Ted never had so much "go" as what I had; he was afraid of Mother and I used to say to him, well, I'm not afraid of Mother, if she whack me, well never mind, I can put up with it. I'm going to do ... what I think I'll do .... Ted would get so worried if I stayed playing at school. It would get a bit dark and he could imagine Mother getting angry ... "You never *will* come home from school properly ... look at the worry if you're out in the dark ..." "I'm not afraid of the dark ..." But he wouldn't go home without me, he'd just wait for me to finish skating or playing or some'ing or other.

We had three miles to walk home and during the winter months we were let out at three o'clock so that we'd be home before dark. Well, one day they kep' us in till three-thirty. They said I was naughty and never paid attention but I don't know. It was a pouring wet day, winter-time, and off we set. We had to go down a dip and then up again. When we got down this dip it was very dark and I must've mistook the turn in the pouring rain and went the other way towards Lower Everleigh instead of going up to Coombe Bake. We walked along and along and along, the rain coming down and it was dark, dark. I wasn't afraid but Ted started to cry. We came to a turnip field and I knew this field was nearly into the wrong village.

I said, "We're going the wrong way! We got to walk back."
Then I heard Mother calling; she was on top of the hill hunting
for us.

"Mother's calling. We got to go back to that voice."

We did. She was cross, oh, she was cross, said it was all my
fault — I always had to put up with that. We got inside the
cottage; she took Ted into the living room. She gave me my
nightdress and I had to undress in the kitchen 'cause we never
undressed in front of one another, never. It was so bitter, bitter
cold. I shall never forget it, and Mother so angry.

"There you are, there's yer cuppa tea and slice of bread and
butter." (We gen'ly had a cooked meal.) "Most likely Ted will
die of pneumonia."

I undressed and went to bed and I never, never forgot how
bitter cold I had been. Dear, dear, dear. I don't think she meant
to be cruel but she'd got in such a state.

Next day she never sent us to school; she went to see the
teacher about keeping us in.

She didn't mean anything wrong to me but you see, I
suppose ... you have all those children — well, day after day,
month in month out, year in year out, and another one coming
— and they were anxious times with these girls away in
service. (Mother had been in service herself and she knew the
dangers) ... all these things made her very strict.

Goodbye to Coombe Bake

At last came the miserable day I'll never forget. A letter came
from Nell saying Billy Gauntlett's wife[14] wanted to see me. I
could have a place looking after her three children, five, seven
and twelve. (I was just fourteen). Mother was pleased ... a good
job in a nice house with no grown-up sons in the family to
chase me (grown-up sons and butlers were her great fear) ... a
good training with other well-trained servants. I told Ted how
I felt about being shut up, never no more running off to see
anything — like soldiers on the march, bands playing, planes

flying. Saying goodbye to him and all the animals. I'd be like a wild thing in a cage!

It was June 1913 and Mother and me went off in the pony cart to Manor Farm, East Grafton, and in we went to see this tall, fair lady. She looked me up and down and asked Mother could I clean a room, make beds and keep everything tidy? 'Course I must be very clean and tidy in myself — was I good-tempered? I'd be under a nursery governess and must do everything that was wanted. I had to have a uniform:

6 white aprons
2 plain grey dresses for morning
1 dark grey dress for afternoon
1 dark grey coat
1 dark grey hat
2 white caps

All this came to £6, a large sum that Mother would have to find. I would start work at 6 o'clock and go on till 9 o'clock at night, must of course go to church every Sunday morning. I'd get one day off a month. For all this I'd get my food and one shilling a week! I said nothing but thought to myself, "I won't stay."

Back home we went and there was Ted.

"How did you get on, Win?"

"Just think, Ted, a shilling a week! I'll have to go, but I'm not staying."

I've lost most of the Wiltshire dialect, but I heard broad Wiltshire not long ago in Devizes and it did sound funny. My mother talked broad Dorset, I s'pose Father did too but he was very particular about how he talked. When I was in service I could talk absolute good Oxford because there were governesses and you found you copied.

Manor Farm, 1929

Taking the Shilling

Nell's husband Jack dropped me and my tin box at the back door of Manor Farm. I looked around for the tall, fair lady but instead out came Cook, fat and important in a blue and white striped apron. She talked broad Wiltshire.

"You're sleepin' with Millie; she's ill in bed today so she can tell you all about everything. Up here now."

Up and up the backstairs till, right at the top of the house, Cook opened a door. The first thing I saw in that attic bedroom was a pale, thin girl with mousy hair, lying in an iron bed. Her name was Millie Green. The room had one small window and no ceiling, only the wooden rafters. On the bare floor was a washstand, jug and basin and the tin box where Millie kept her outdoor clothes. I was to share the small bed with her and our sheets, I soon found out, was made of flour bags washed and sewn together.

Millie told me later how she envied me my fair hair and blue eyes that first day we met. But from the day I started wearing those white caps my hair got darker and darker till by the time I left service it was deep brown.

Millie was housemaid and parlourmaid rolled into one. She had to start her day carrying cans of water upstairs, cleaning and polishing, rushing round to get all her rough work done by eleven. On the dot of eleven she must be changed out of her print dress into her black parlourmaid's dress with white cap and apron, ready to take the Lady's coffee in. (In service, you usually talked of your employer as "The Lady.") The rest of her day would be spent answering the door, laying tables, waiting at them, clearing away, running errands, making up the fires, anything that cropped up. Like me, she had a shilling a week and her keep. She was a poor little thing, never seemed very strong to me, and she did die young.

Besides Cook, Millie and me, there were two more on the indoor staff. One was Miss Gummery, the nursery governess, the other was Billy Barnes.

Billie was what they called the "houseboy". He had to clean the passage that did go out to the front door, the front doorstep and grates, scrub floors, and other dirty jobs. When he'd finished indoors Nell's Jack (he was foreman for the two farms, this one and the one at Collingbourne) would have work for him on the land.

Miss Gummery seemed elderly to me but p'raps she was only forty; a thick-bodied, spreading sort of woman in a tight-fitting black dress with a lace collar. I could see I must be "just so" with her.

I don't remember feeling shy on that first day. I s'pose I was a bit homesick but I knew the sooner I got on with things the sooner I'd find a way out. My first job was taking the two younger children, Sonny and Doreen, out for a drive. Billy told me the grey pony in the orchard was the one to use with the trap and I was expected to do the rest. Just as well I was used to putting a pony in the shafts at home.

After the drive and their tea they had to be bathed and made neat and tidy ready for six o'clock prayers. There was no hot water taps in the house and I had to carry the bath hot water in two big cans filled from kettles on the kitchen range. I managed to bath Doreen quite well and then it was Sonny's turn. When I undressed him it was the first time I'd seen what a boy looked like with nothing on. After I'd washed him he wouldn't get out of the bath. When I tried to lift him he did splash and made me wet through so't I had to rush afterwards and get my apron dry in time for prayers. And he did do that every night, obstinate little boy.

The Family Prayers was not very friendly or family-like to

me. We trooped into the dining room and the children went and stood with their mother and father by the table. Olive, the twelve-year-old, was with them, a handsome dark-haired girl. We servants stood the other side and all very solemn, no good evening or anything. Mr. Gauntlett, big, dark-haired, grumpy-looking, led the Lord's Prayer, then a reading from the Bible, prayers again and that was the end. No goodnights.

Next morning Millie and I were up at six, washed in cold water we'd carried up, struggled into our starchy uniforms. After breakfast in the kitchen I learned the routines for every day. Olive went to school in Marlborough and I had to get her ready, brush her hair and see she was all right to catch the train; then take the young ones' breakfast to the nursery — porridge, milk and egg. At nine o'clock, Mrs. Gauntlett sent for me to the drawing room. Everything seemed very grand, the thick carpet, huge fireside rug, bright copper fender and fire irons, a grand piano, bowls of flowers on little tables, all the furniture gleaming from Millie's elbow grease. My mistress was in her morning dress, a fine dark skirt to her toes and a beautiful cream-coloured blouse with a high neck and lace down the front. Even sitting down she looked very tall, with her fair hair in a big bun on top.

"Good morning, Winifred."

She was always very polite, but never asked how you were or noticed if you had a cold or anything. You was a maid and you looked after yourself from the moment you left home. The cook, nor no-one never took any notice. But I never was ill, worried or depressed. There was never no time for that.

"Yes, Madam."

I don't know what instructions she gave that day, but that was always the answer. Perhaps I was told to take the children out to tea somewhere (if so, I'd have my own tea in the servants' quarters) or just for a drive, or to bring them to the drawing room if there was visitors.

After me, Millie got her orders for the day and then Cook. If Mrs. Gauntlett wanted to be driven anywhere, the head groom would have to be told.

After I'd seen Mrs. Gauntlett Miss Gummery told me about my special extra duties for each day. It went something like this: Mondays — help with the children's washing; Tuesdays — children's ironing; Wednesday — clean their bedrooms and bathroom; Thursday — clean the backstairs (the children had to use the back, like us servants); Fridays might be sewing. Miss Gummery's sister did come in and do all the children's sewing but I had to tack everything ready. While I was doing this Sonny and Doreen had lessons with their governess.

That afternoon I glimpsed Mrs. Gauntlett going in from the garden. She'd changed into a gorgeous mauve muslin with frills at the neck. I s'pose she wore corsets underneath but I only looked at the lovely dress. Then the bell rang for Millie to take tea in. Tea in those days was an important meal, very carefully served with a lace cloth, special cakes, thin bread and butter and jam.

Sometimes they wanted clotted cream for tea and that meant a trip to the dairy. This was a big square building and inside a big copper was always bubbling. The churns were stored in a rack and near the copper was a big stone trough or sink where they were all washed and scalded. The stone floor was completely scrubbed every day, the water running down a drain in the middle. Then there was this cooler. Cold water was kept running down one side of it and on the other side the milk was poured from buckets and strained through cloths. These cloths was boiled every day and everything was sterilised that could be.

Now about the clotted cream. If the drawing room wanted it, Cook was responsible for making it, but cream for the children was my job. Every night I poured milk into enamel basins and left these on the kitchen stove all night. In the morning I did skim off the yellow top into a dish and when it had cooled there was your clotted cream to go with their strawberry jam.

The skimmed milk from that cream might be fed to pigs in the village, or more often it was used up in the kitchen for our meals. We seldom had the same food as what the dining room had. If they had steamed chickens we had soup made from the water but we never saw a bit of chicken. Sometimes hares came in to be cooked and again we'd have soup from them, but we never had none of the meat.

And yet the Gauntletts were so wealthy; they farmed land from Great Bedwyn right down to Collingbourne Kingston.

Billy Gauntlett's farm at East Grafton and his father's at Collingbourne were run together, with Jack Smith (Nell's husband) as foreman at both. I gradually got to know the outside staff at East Grafton. The head groom — I forget his name — looked after Mr. Gauntlett's horses and if the lady wanted to be driven anywhere he would harness one to her trap. He would never dream of touching the children's pony or Miss Olive's horse. That job was for the second groom, who happened to be his nephew, Fred Grace. Fred was three years older than me, a nice-looking lad with dark hair, not very tall. His father was a milker at the farm, and all his five brothers worked there at different times (William Grace worked in the Gauntletts' smithy and when war broke out joined the artillery as a farrier.)

After the grooms came the carters that looked after the horses for the plough: head carter, under-carter and third carter — that would be a lad straight from school. Then you had head cowman (a Mr. Clarke) second cowman and under him two or three men working in the milking sheds. Then there were two shepherds and a man looking after the poultry and collecting the eggs. Daymen were employed in the fields at certain seasons and to help with the sheep. They employed all these men and us in the house and I don't suppose the whole lot cost them a hundred pounds.[14]

Billy Barnes was walking out with Millie, I soon found out, and I used to tease them both. I'd wait till no-one was about, get behind Billy, rough up his hair and dance round him singing "Billy and Millie, Millie and Billy" ... He got really worried in case Cook heard. Years later he told me he was always afraid of what I would do next. One afternoon he came into the kitchen. The children had gone out somewhere and I was supposed to be darning socks.

"Don't worry, I know all about you two. They're gone out and Millie's taken the sewing up into the summer house and she's waiting for you to go and kiss her!"

"Not likely, with you spying on us!"

"Ah, well, I might."

I never caught them cuddling or kissing, I expect Millie was too scared of all that, like most of us. She was brought up stiff and starchy all right, and she didn't have no go in her, poor girl. I didn't get many socks darned that day.

One morning when I was alone in the nursery I heard a sharp whistle. Our window looked down over the stables. I looked out and there was Fred Grace grinning and waving. I laughed and waved back. I thought it would be fun to tease him like I did Billy, but I never had nothing else in mind. He was beginning to take notice of me and I s'pose I encouraged him, being only fourteen and knowing nothing about how men felt. The next day I heard him singing:

Blue bells I gather
Take them and be true
When I'm a man, my plan
Will be to marry you.

"No fear! I'm not marrying anybody!"

My work was really with Doreen and Sonny, not with Olive except for odd things like making her bed, brushing her hair. Hair-brushing, that was the time I had to watch out — she'd kick me if she got the chance. What a little Madam, always made it clear she looked down on me. If she could put me down she would.

Every Saturday Fred brought round her beautiful black horse for her to go riding with her father. She looked very smart in her divided skirt with her shiny black curls swinging round her face. One wet Saturday after her ride she came into the kitchen in boots with mud nearly up to the knee.

"Winifred, take my boots off."

"No."

"Take them off at once or I'll tell Mamma."

"All right, tell Mamma."

Cook looked very worried and whispered, "You'd better do it, you'll get the sack else." I ignored this. Olive fumed.

"Millie, tell Mamma I want to see her."

Off goes Millie, but Mrs. Gauntlett sent her back saying why was Olive in the kitchen asking for her mother.

"Tell Mamma Winifred won't take my dirty boots off."

In the end Mamma came and told Olive she should've had them taken off outside, but she snapped at me, "Why wouldn't you take Miss Olive's boots off?"

"Because of the way Miss Olive spoke to me."

Olive stamped her foot and went out and Mrs. Gauntlett said no more, but Cook and Millie were horrified and sure I'd get the sack. But I never, and anyway I wasn't going to let her boss me around. Respect for employers was one thing, cheek from their children another.

My shilling a week was paid monthly, four shillings every four weeks until my sixteenth birthday in 1915. At the end of that May my pay slip said "4/- less . .... (so many pence)". Cook said "That's because you're paying insurance now." Even so I was doing better than Nell had — she never got more than sixpence a week. But I kept my ears open in case any other jobs were going.

I never had no holiday from East Grafton, and when Christmas came it was just like an ordinary Sunday. The Gauntletts themselves didn't do much about it, and we never had no present or extra money. It was then that I felt it very much being away from home and missed Ted and Mother and Dad. For two years I didn't see them at all unless anyone was going to Collingbourne from the farm on my day off. Then if Mother knew in time she'd go to Nell's and meet me there and someone would drop me back at eight in the evening.

On Sunday the whole household went to church. It was just across the road and I had to get the children ready in their best clothes, take them down to the hall to go with their parents. We gave the family time to get settled in their pew and then Cook, Millie and I went across and sat in the opposite pew, not the same side as the gentry. That was the usual custom for servants. After the service Millie and I waited till they'd all gone out and there outside would be Fred and the village lads. (Fred's home was in East Grafton.) I don't know if they'd been in church or not but they did tease us girls as usual.

Millie and I got on all right together. We shared the day's grind and dropped thankfully into our attic beds at night. We never fell out, grumbled about anything or even bothered to talk much — that would've been a waste of good sleeping time. On Saturday nights we were allowed to have a hot bath — in the laundry. We carried the hot water from the dairy next door and took it in turns, first Cook, then Millie, then me, locking ourselves in. It was cold getting out on to the stone floor, but we was used to that. After all, we wasn't cuddled up at home.

It was a hard life but I do think we learned a lot from our work, for instance, how to run a home. Everything had to be strictly to time and just so, and it made you be disciplined in all sides of your life. That was why Mother was so keen to see her girls got good places in service. It was a kind of education. And I suppose we maids made good wives — strong ones anyway!

One Sunday at the beginning of August 1914 I went home for my day off. Mother and I went over to Beach's Barn where Jane lived — she'd been married to George Ferris and living there about four years. You could often find mushrooms in the meadows round there and three of us went to look for some early ones. An Army sergeant came through the gate and asked if we minded him looking for mushrooms too. While we were all strolling round he suddenly said:

"Shan't be doing this much longer by the look of things.

Heard the news?"

"No, what?"

"Germany have invaded Belgium and if they don't back out we'll all be off to France to fight."

We hadn't known anything out of the ordinary was going on. News didn't spread very fast then, with newspapers only getting to us a day late, being so far from the town and no wireless of course. But after all, soldiers was always coming and going on the Plain and this was just another bit of army business to us.

When I got back to East Grafton I did hear them talking about a war starting but no-one was worried or at all excited. Whatever it was was happening far away and I soon forgot about it.

One day I met Billy in the dairy. It was late autumn, 1914 and the Great War was on.

"Fred's coming in to get some hot water. Got a sick horse."

Now for a bit of fun, I thought. I got a bucket o' cold water, stood on a stool behind the open door and waited. I heard footsteps and as they reached the door I emptied my bucket over the top, Oh, the swearing! Not in Fred's voice, but the head cowman's. He raged and yelled for Cook and "Oh, what's she done, Mr. Clarke? How dare you, you bad girl. I ought to thrash you. You do somethin' like that again and I'll tell the Lady. Get back to work at once."

I said I was sorry and she took him off to the kitchen to dry his clothes. Then Fred came in laughing — he'd seen it all.

"Won't be able to tease me much longer, Win, I've volunteered for the Army."

Did he know I was fascinated by soldiers? Anyrate, I was impressed, I didn't know that he'd volunteered twice before: he was fed up with the Gauntletts grumbling about his work and thought he'd be better off taking the King's shilling. Both times he went to Pewsey for the medical and had failed it — no-one knew why. I think his nerves must have been bad. This time they passed him and one Monday morning in January

1915 Billy told me Fred had his calling up papers. This was before the big recruiting drive when Kitchener's finger was pointing at everyone from a poster saying "Your Country Needs You", but already young men from the villages were going every day. I thought I'd go and wish Fred luck when he came to the back door for his pay — "five shillings with cap off"! When I saw the men all lined up I went down, with my milk jug as an excuse, towards the dairy. Fred stopped me, blushing to his neat, dark head and told me he had to report at Devizes the next day.

"Will you write to me, Win?"

"Drop me a line first and then I might."

I'll never forget how his face lit up then. But then I went off all unconcerned to get my milk. I liked him a lot, but I didn't want to be serious with him or anybody. I wasn't sixteen yet and besides Mother had done her work of frightening me off.

I heard later that when he went for his money that day Jack Smith told him they wasn't going to pay him because he shouldn't have volunteered when the farm needed him. Same with his brothers when they volunteered, they didn't get no pay. Employers were all trying to hang on to their men. And the Gauntletts said they'd sack his elderly father and throw him out of his cottage because his sons had gone. But Fred had been in the Navy as a boy and he'd learned a bit about his rights. So when he got to Devizes he told the C.O. and in the end the Army saw he got his pay from the Gauntletts and that his father was kept on. But the Gauntletts didn't forget, and after the war when he wanted a reference they wouldn't give him one.

The day after Fred left I met Mr. Clarke in the dairy.

"I'm going to write to Fred Grace in the Army," I said, proud of my soldier friend.

"Huh, I wouldn't let a girl of mine have anything to do with him. You don't know what a bad lad he was when he was young. After his mother died when he was eleven no-one could do anything with him. His father strapped him, that didn't do any good so they asked the vicar. The vicar said

"Right! Uncontrollable boy like that, the only thing that will bring him to his senses is send him in the Navy. And he were sent when he were thirteen. A real bad lot, that boy."

"Well," I said, "He's good enough for me."

There was a Belgian refugee girl there that the Gauntletts had taken on for dairy work. She decided to butt in.

"Pooh! English soldiers never any good!"

"I'll show you who's any good!"

I just went mad, jumped at her, scratched and punched her. She had lovely long hair I could hold on to, and I pulled it and wouldn't let go. She screamed and Mr. Clarke ran for Cook. Oh, didn't she get in a state!

"What're we goin' to do with her? Leave off at once, you wicked girl. You're getting worse every day. Look at your hair, and your cap hangin' half-off. It's no good, I'll 'ave to tell Nell and she'll tell your Mother."

"I don't care, I'm not staying much longer anyway."

I wasn't. A month or two later I had a letter from Millie who'd left Gauntlett's in 1914. She was working now in Speen, near Newbury and there was a job going in the same house if I wanted to apply for it. A Mrs. Burton was looking for a nanny to look after three children and a new baby that was expected soon. I'd get a half-day off every Thursday and every other Sunday *and* a fortnight's holiday a year, and much better wages — five shillings a week. So I wrote to this Mrs. Burton and she agreed to take me on, subject to a satisfactory reference.

But there were more battles to fight before I could leave East Grafton. Just getting to give in your notice was difficult. In those days you couldn't get to see The Lady straight off. I asked Cook's permission and she said, "No, you can't see her." So then I asked the parlourmaid (the one that took over from Millie) if I could follow her in when she went through to "the front." Mrs. Gauntlett saw me coming in and asked what I was doing there.

"I want to give a month's notice, please Madam."

"That's out of the question. Your mother would never hear

of it."

"Well, I'm going."

"You certainly are not. We're very satisfied with you. I shall tell your brother-in-law to tell his wife to write to your mother. She'll put a stop to it."

Next time I went to Collingbourne on my half-day, Mother was there in a state about it all.

"You can't leave a good job like that. It's your living."

"I've got a better job, near Newbury."

"Newbury! You cant go there — it's full o' troops, all coming down from Stockcross ... no-one to keep an eye on you ... whatever would you do ..."

"I can look after myself, Mother."

She cried and carried on, Nell was really nasty about it, but I'd made up my mind.

Mrs. Gauntlett did everything to try and stop me — I were good with children and she knew it. When it came to sending a reference she wrote that I was a very good worker, but she had just one little thing against me — I wasn't strictly to the truth. Cook had told her this because of a kettle I was supposed to fill with fresh water every day; one day I said I'd done it and Cook said "I know you never." Well — that was true — I'd only topped the water up! But I was still offered the job.

At last one morning Mrs. Gauntlett asked was I still going to leave. I said yes.

"I can only hope you'll behave yourself in Newbury."

Miss Gummery was rather nice that day, very sorry to see me go after two years under her.

"You're such a good girl, Winifred. But you have some serious faults, you know," she said sadly. I s'pose someone had told her about the teasing and playing about.

At the end of August I asked the man that did take the milk to the station if he'd take me and my box too.

I'd taken my last shilling from Manor Farm.

Winifred

Billy Barnes had left Gauntletts' that year too. He went to work at Marlborough College as a pantry boy. There he worked his way up to waiter, then head waiter. He'd volunteered several times for the Army at the beginning of the war, but they kept turning him down at his medical. There was a housemaid at the College wanted him to marry her, so she went and told the matron she was expecting Billy's baby. You often heard this sort of thing in service — sometimes it was true, sometimes not. Anyrate, Billy wasn't having that. He had one more go at volunteering and this time they took him 'cause they were getting short of men by then. He came through the war all right and did marry Millie Green. We all met up again when I was married too, after the war.

A Wider World

"Keep away from all those soldiers, mind ..... and I shall write to the Lady and tell her not to let you have too much time off to run around Newbury ...."

I promised to write every week and the train carried me away from Collingbourne Station and Mother's worried face. I'd made a decision of my own in spite of her and I was determined it would work.

When I got to Speen there was Millie waiting to take me down to the drawing room to meet the Lady. It all seemed very different from East Grafton. Here was Mrs. Burton, a big, homely lady, taking my hand, asking kindly about my journey and introducing Colin, Michael and Diana. They were seven, six and three. The new baby was expected in a few weeks. They soon dragged me off to the nursery to have tea. At the table, Michael piped up first.

"Can I have a sugar lump?"

Better be careful, I thought. Sugar was already short, although not rationed yet.

"Are you allowed one?"

"Oh yes, but Colin isn't."

"Why not?" I already felt sorry for Colin because he had a cast in his eye and had to wear special glasses.

"Our other Nanny didn't let him, she liked me best."

So, she'd spoilt Michael because he was better-looking I supposed. I wasn't going to favour him. They all got a sugar lump and I told Michael he'd go in the corner if he was unkind. He glared at me.

"I never go in the corner."

"You will if you deserve it."

Michael sulked a bit after this, but he soon came round and in a few days he was all charm. "We're going to call you "Rose" because you look just like one."

Everything felt more friendly here, and although the Burtons were very wealthy — he was a busy auctioneer — they only kept a small staff. Besides Millie there was a gardener and of course a cook, but no nursery governess over me. I was to be Nanny, in charge of everything to do with the children, and trusted. It was a big step up and made me keen to do the job well. I settled down more willingly than I had at the Gauntletts. All my meals would be with the children and, thank goodness, no family prayers.

But although the Burtons were good and fair employers for those days, they were as strict as most others and very much "up there." Mr. Burton, a small ginger-haired man, never took any notice of me except a gruff "Good Morning". Mrs. Burton was nice enough but she always kept her distance. I know she liked me. (I discovered how much many years later) but it would never have done to seem to favour one servant more than the others. And I may have been "Our Rose" to the children but I had to remember that, like with their parents, I was on one plane and they were on another. Servants mustn't be allowed over that gap. It had to be "Master Colin", "Master Michael", and "Miss Diana." I'd been taught by Miss Gummery too that you mustn't make a lot of fuss of them and never, never kiss or cuddle them. If they fell down and cried, you just said, "Come along now, you haven't hurt yourself." Their Mother wouldn't like it if you tried to take her place.

The house at Speen was not specially grand but there was one thing that made my work easier. It had hot and cold water laid on in the bathroom and cloakroom. No more struggling up dozens of stairs with cans of scalding water.

Otherwise my duties were much like at East Grafton. One thing I remember is that besides having an English and a music teacher, Colin and Michael had French lessons some afternoons. The French teacher used to stay to tea and she made us speak French all through the meal — me as well as the children. I picked up quite a bit and I dare say if I'd met that Belgian refugee again I could have told her in French not to insult "soldats d'Angleterre"!

In October 1915 Baby Pauline was born and a private nurse came. Better-off people always had this "monthly nurse" to look after mother and baby for the first four weeks. After that I was called in to help. Mrs. Burton liked to bath little Pauline herself but I got the bath ready and the feed, looked after the pram and cot, and of course I washed the nappies. I gradually did more and more for the baby and I did get rather fond of her.

As things turned out, Millie wasn't with us at Speen much longer. She went home for her fortnight's holiday and when it was nearly time to come back she wrote and asked if she could stay home a bit longer. (The Burtons didn't have a telephone at that time.) Millie's brother had come on leave from France and she wanted to see something of him. No, said the Burtons, and soon we had a new maid.

When she arrived I found she was from near home, from Everleigh. She was a bit younger than me but I could just remember Hilda Faye at school; she used to live down the Marlborough Road, a lovely looking girl with beautiful long dark curls, really smashing. I looked forward to going out with her when we had time off.

Meanwhile it was nearly Christmas and I began to feel homesick as usual. It was too far to go home on half days and except for my yearly holiday I was never there during my eight years with the Burtons. This year, 1915, we all went off, that is, the Burtons and children and me to look after them, to spend Christmas with Mrs. Burton's parents. Mr. and Mrs. Simmons lived near Basingstoke and it was their custom to give each of their staff half a crown in an envelope as a Christmas present. That year I got one, and Mrs. Burton did give her staff something too, for Christmas. She gave me a uniform dress — that was what you usually got in service, either a ready-made dress or a length of material to make one, or perhaps an apron.

I wasn't sorry to get back to Speen, especially as there was a letter there to cheer me up. I guessed it was from Fred because of the good clear handwriting. His education as a lad in the Navy had done that for him. I somehow knew that he would go on writing to me whenever he could. It couldn't be regular because you never knew with army posts, men moving about, going on active service and mail being destroyed. I liked his letters, always matter-of-fact and uncomplaining; and nothing silly in them, like about love. (I thought that would be silly because I was afraid of it.)

It was not till summer 1916 that I heard again. He was home at East Grafton on leave, said that neat hand-writing, and could he come and see me on my half-day? Mother, it seemed, had heard about this and said it would be all right. True, he was a soldier but she knew the family and felt she could trust him. So on my next Thursday I arranged to meet him in Newbury. I was free from three in the afternoon until nine.

Fred seemed just the same, or perhaps not quite — more of a grown-up man, was that it? He was twenty now and that seemed a mature age to me. He didn't say anything about the war or what it was like at the Front. I know now that his regiment, the Wiltshires, had been in the terrible battle of the Somme that began on July 1st. We didn't know, but hundreds of thousands had been killed or maimed there. No wonder Fred looked older.

We had tea in Newbury and strolled round the town. He seemed thrilled to be with me but I was glad there was still no flirting or love talk. I couldn't go out with him again else, much too scared of any man getting close to me. If a man tried to do that it meant he didn't respect you, Mother had said. But I didn't mind being gently kissed after he'd walked me home to Speen.

I saw him once more before he went back. I knew it was to France because he had to report to Dover.

"Goodbye, Win. Keep smiling."

I cried a bit then. I wasn't in love or anything like that, but he was my best friend and he was going into danger.

In August 1916 the Burtons arranged to take the children to Scotland and I was told to have my fortnight's holiday then. You never had no choice about your holiday time. When sister Maggie heard I'd be free she asked Mother if I could spend the time with her in London, looking after Heidi and Betty again. Mother said yes, so of course that was that — off I went. All I remember of that fortnight is Maggie waking me up one morning, very excited and scared.

"A German Zeppelin come over in the night. They say it dropped bombs somewhere!"

All that day people were talking about it, this huge German airship, like a great silver fish in the sky. The papers were full of it and there were photos of the damage it'd done.

There were more air raids to come, first by Zepps and then aeroplanes. The war suddenly became real to me. If people in London could be in danger, how much worse it must be to be fighting. After that I got into the habit of looking at the casualty lists, after I was back at Speen. Names of the wounded and dead was published every day in rank order — Majors, Captains, Lieutenants, Sergeant Majors, Sergeants — right down to privates, with each man's army number. People with sons, husbands or sweethearts at the Front were always looking at these lists and now I used to look to make sure Fred's name wasn't there, nor Billie Barnes', nor anyone I knew.

Life in Newbury was much more fun than East Grafton and Hilda and I were off to the town as often as we could. It was a three-mile walk. Most entertainments were put on in the evenings so sometimes we asked for the evening off instead of the afternoon. We often went to what they called a "Fur and Feather" whist drive. The first prize would be a pheasant, second prize perhaps two partridges and the third three hares. A rabbit was booby prize. I don't remember ever winning anything — who'd have cooked the thing if I had!

One evening there was a big Fair in the grounds of one of

the big houses. It was to raise money to build a new hospital near Reading. There was to be a band, a military display and all sorts of side-shows. Hilda and I got permission to go and stay out till ten o'clock. The gardener would pick us up at the gate at ten.

Off we went in our best dresses and the first thing we went for was the swing boats, and in the next swing were two soldiers. Would we like to pair off with them for a swing? All right, we said and then they took us off for a cup of tea. I paid for my own (Never accept anything from a stranger, said Mother.) It turned out they were from Tidworth so then we told them we were from Salisbury Plain. Then we got talking about horses and that led to a visit to the stables of the big house. We chattered, time passed and I realised it must be getting late. It was a quarter to ten.

"Come on Hilda. we've got to be at the gate by ten."

"I'm not bothered about the time, Win."

"Well, I'm going. He'll be at the gate and you know we'll get the sack if we're not there."

"Oh, never mind that."

I said goodnight and hurried to the gate. When the gardener came we waited for Hilda and she didn't turn up for ages and ages. When at last we got home Mr. Burton was waiting for us.

"What's the meaning of this? What kept you?"

The gardener told him and the next morning Hilda was on the mat and off she had to go without a reference. It was silly of her because once you started not having references you could only get what they did call "low class" jobs, like being a general maid somewhere where there was no other staff and even that you'd be lucky to get. If you wanted to get on, the only way was to work your way up carefully and steadily by getting good references. Even a kitchenmaid could do this. She might start with cleaning vegetables, washing up and cleaning round after the cook, then she might get a better kitchenmaid's job. If one day the cook was ill then she'd have the chance to take over. Then if she did all right and that cook left, the kitchenmaid might move up into the cook's job, then one day perhaps be cook-housekeeper. You had to watch your step, not upset anybody and keep your eye open for opportunities.

I don't know where Hilda went after she left but after her there came a girl called Mabel Tanner. Oh, Mabel Tanner! She wasn't with us long and no wonder. She was a tall redhead, not all that pretty but her hair was gorgeous. One half-day she

Mabel

went to Reading. Why to Reading? She didn't have no rela-
tives or nothing there and I don't know how she travelled
there but she came back with a lovely new coat, a dark tweed
with fur collar. Well, you couldn't get a coat like that on our
wage without a lot of saving up. I asked where she got it. Oh,
she said, if she wanted anything she knew what to do.

"But how did you get it?"

"I met an officer and I told him the price of the coat and he
said it was all right."

"Mabel! You never went and did that?"

"Oh yes, when I want something I go all out and get it."

I was terrible shocked and said wasn't she afraid of having
a baby. Well, she went home soon after and didn't come back;
whether she had a baby or not I don't know.

I found out that quite a lot of this sort of thing went on.
There was one maid we knew and she went down in the
marshes by the river with an Australian. Then she came back,
he walked on and she said something about he gave her a good
price. She never went back into service no more but earned her
living like that, got herself a house in Newbury, never married, but earned enough to keep herself comfortably. She came
from the back streets of Newbury so I suppose she wanted an
easier life. Some girls were driven to it. But Mabel Tanner
wasn't driven to it — she come from a good home in Chippen-
ham.

I was meeting all kinds of people and learning fast about
life. I began to understand why Mother worried who I made
friends with. She needn't have. Mostly they were girls working in the big houses around and all we did was meet in a cafe
for a cup of tea and a chat, or go to the 'pictures' at sixpence a
time.

There was one friend I made that wasn't in service. Her name
was Dolly Adams and she was in munitions. One day she
asked if I'd like to come to tea at her grandparents', near
Donnington Castle. The castle was a ruin and all that was left
of it was two huge towers and a gateway covered in ivy,

standing on a green. The grandparents were something to do with the place — perhaps their job was to look after the grass and surroundings. I don't quite remember, but Dolly said her cousin in the Australian army would be there and a friend of his. I liked going out anywhere so of course I went, on my Sunday half-day. This was early summer, 1917.

The grandparents were friendly and I enjoyed the teatime, with Dolly's cousin chattering on about Australia. His friend Ron Baker was sitting quiet and I had a look at him. He was rather short and viking-fair but quite ordinary I thought. They were both stationed at Larkhill.

When it was time for me to go back to Speen this Ron asked if he could walk back with me. I said yes, I'd be glad of the company and he got up to get his hat, the Anzac's broad brimmed bush hat they wore. Their uniforms were almost like our soldiers' but the jacket had no turn-down collar.

We said goodbye to the others and started down the road. The evening sun wrapped me round and I felt happy.

It was a wonderful walk. We talked non-stop. About Salisbury Plain and all its landmarks, and about army manoeuvres. Ron was astonished and mystified about how I could know all that, until I told him where my home was. He asked did I never go home nowadays? Yes, I was going there very soon for my fortnight's holiday. Ron looked thoughtful and I went on to tell him all about my family and how hard everyone had to work, and about my time at East Grafton. Then he told me what had been happening to him.

He was twenty-four and had been wounded at Gallipoli. He was still fighting the memory of it.

"My brother was with me ... just a few yards in front when he fell down. There was fighting all round and I couldn't get to him to see if he was dead ... didn't dare try. He must've been killed but I've never heard ... It was hell..."

This was the most terrible story I'd heard about the war. I wanted to say I was sorry but could only run on about Larkhill, Tidworth and the different regiments (I knew them all). Ron asked when I'd be at Coombe Bake for my holiday and we arranged to meet in the woods on my first evening.

All the next week I puzzled how I could get to meet Ron — Mother would have a fit if she knew. Going to see Jane, that was it. Jane and George lived at Beach's Barn, the other side of the woods so that ought to satisfy Mother. The night before I went home I dreamt I went there, walked all around for hours but Ron never came. Perhaps he wouldn't.

But that evening in the woods I saw the short khaki figure in the broad-brimmed hat leaning against a tree. My heart jumped as Ron ran towards me, almost shouting with delight.

"Three cheers! You're really here. I was afraid you wouldn't come ... dreamt you didn't turn up."

How strange that was, but it made me feel very much at home with him. We walked again, and carried on talking as we had before. Ron's life was full of interest to me. I heard about a world that was new and exciting — Broome, in North-West Australia. His father had been a pearl merchant in Scotland and Ron was born there. His grandmother still lived in Perth but the rest of the family had emigrated when his father found out he could make more money in Australia for the pearl business. For instance they could employ Chinese boys for the diving because they could stay under water longer. I was fascinated to hear all this and about how the family started out from scratch; how, before they could do anything they had to build huts to sleep in, one for the father and mother, one for Ron's sister and one for him and his two brothers. Real pioneers they were.

I knew of one or two poor families in Wiltshire that had emigrated to try and make a better life and I rather liked the idea myself, so I was happy to listen to all this.

I did listen every evening for the rest of my fortnight, Ron walking the eight miles from Larkhill and getting someone to do his guard duty for him so we could meet. The memory of that fortnight is still precious to me. And even Mother couldn't have objected to anything Ron said or did when we met. He actually said I was "almost too pretty to kiss." We would write and perhaps one day — who knew?

After my holiday I got back to Speen to find a postcard from Fred marked "On Active Service", and stamped "Army Post Office." The Salvation Army did issue these cards to men at the Front at times when they couldn't manage to write letters. The card said; "I'm fighting fit. Looking forward to seeing you soon. Love, Fred." I sent back a friendly letter.

The next day there was a letter in a new handwriting — from Larkhill. How I treasured that letter and the ones that came every day until Ron was sent abroad. In the last of them he said that he loved me, but he was in rather low spirits. The reason was he'd been to call on my parents. He wanted to meet them and let them see he was all right, that they needn't worry about us knowing each other.

"But it didn't turn out like that. Your Dad was outside and I had a bit of a chat with him," said Ron's letter, "but then your mother called him in, shouted something about setting the dogs on me and slammed the door."

Oh dear, I should have warned him. We'd have to wait.

It was hard to think about anything but Ron at this time but I soon had to. Illness came to the Burton family.

On the Saturday after I got back from my holiday I was told to have the children all ready by nine o'clock the next morning to go to the grandparents at Basingstoke for the day. Well, on the Sunday morning, little Pauline said her head ached and then she was very sick. I didn't like the look of her and told the Lady I didn't think she ought to go out anywhere. Mrs. Burton thought I was making a fuss about nothing, but they did leave her behind with me. She got worse as the day went on and I was worried. I knew there was a military nurse working up the road so I sent to ask if she would come down and see Pauline. She took one look and sent for the doctor. I heard the word "diphtheria" and before long two nurses were in the room, and they were going on about disinfecting. All the carpets had to come up, I had to scrub the floor and everything in the room with carbolic. A big sheet boiled in onion water was hung over the door to keep the germs from getting out.

93

When the family got back from Basingstoke there was a to-do. The other children were sent straight back to the grandparents for safety. A day nurse and a night nurse were got in for Pauline, one of them always to be on duty. No-one else was to go near, not even the parents. One morning one of the nurses asked me if I'd be afraid to go into the sickroom. Pauline couldn't speak but they thought she wanted me. They'd been trying to feed her through a tube but she kept shaking her head. I went in and spoke to her and they gave me a bowl of warm milk with a little Bovril; one end of a tube was in the bowl and Pauline let me put the other end in her mouth and she did begin to drink through it. I did this every day, putting on a disinfected overall and leaving it in the room afterwards. As she got a little better we gave her milk thickened with boiled oatmeal.

The doctor had to find out how she caught the illness and first they had the sanitary people to look at the drains, but then at Basingstoke one day Michael told them about the trough.

While I'd been away on holiday they'd had a temporary nanny and she'd taken the children to a part of Speen where there was a large horse trough. It hadn't been used for some time but water had been left standing in it. While the nanny was gossiping Pauline paddled her hands in the water, Michael remembered. So they called the sanitary people in again, took some water from the trough and later the diphtheria germs were found in this water. The doctor thought Pauline must have sucked her fingers and got the infection that way. After that they took the trough away or destroyed it.

It was touch and go with Pauline and she was isolated for three weeks. When my mother heard about the diphtheria she wrote in a panic saying I was to come home at once, because she was afraid of losing me like she had the other three. I didn't tell her I'd been in the room with Pauline, just said I couldn't come home and that I'd be all right. The illness did pass but it left Pauline with a weak heart and I had to take extra care of her after that.

1917 dragged on, a long, hard year. It seemed as if the war would never end. Rumours got round that food was running out and it was true that some foods were hard to get, sugar and meat for instance. Rationing hadn't come in yet, and when it did it wasn't well organised like it was in the second world war. Things weren't shared out properly between the various areas. Some well-off people panicked and bought up huge quantities so others went short, but the Burtons were very decent. They didn't buy on the black market and they shared everything they got with us. As Mr. Burton often had to go to farms on business he sometimes came home with a chicken, a few eggs or a bit of butter; other times we had to make do with lentil pie or soup made with what bones the butcher could spare.

The casualty lists rolled on. I was afraid for Ron but didn't expect to see his name among the British lists. Australia House issued their lists separately. Then one day I had a letter in an Active Service envelope.

"Dearest Angel, I think about you all the time...."

I wrote back at once, care of Australia House.

I never told anyone about Ron, not Cook or any of the girls from the big houses. You could never be sure they wouldn't tell someone and then it would get to The Lady and she might write to your mother and there'd be trouble. Ron was too important to me and I kept quiet.

Then suddenly I had another letter from Ron, posted in Kent. He was on sick leave getting over a shrapnel wound in his back but it wasn't serious and he would come up to Newbury for the week-end. I thought it out and quickly sent him a postcard — Yes, I could see him on my Sunday half-day. How the week dragged. It was an age since I'd seen him, had he changed? Would we feel the same?

We did. Things seemed more urgent, he'd been wounded again and you never knew what dangers he might face or when we'd see each other again. He was full of the idea we should get married before he went back. He could afford to marry, he said, and he could provide for me in case he got killed. Would I go up to Scotland with him and meet his grandmother? We could be married straight away from there.

I was in a turmoil. What could I say? I wasn't twenty-one and how could I marry without asking Mother. And I knew what she would say. I couldn't go against her in this, my upbringing had been too strong and perhaps I didn't have the courage.

"No, Ron," I said sadly. "You go and see your grandmother alone and when you come back we'll see."

Before we parted he gave me a gold brooch shaped like the map of Australia, set with little diamonds where the map goes into points. We couldn't arrange to meet again — I wasn't due for a Sunday half-day for another fortnight and I'd had my mid-week half-day in advance. He walked back to Speen with me, kissed me. There didn't seem to be anything else to say. I ran into the house.

I don't know whether he went to Scotland or not. I had one more letter from "somewhere in England" saying he had to rejoin his regiment. He couldn't say where, of course. He would write when he could.

I wrote back, care of Australia House, and after a while wrote again, and then again after a few weeks but no answer came. I watched summer shrink into autumn. Then one day Cook said there was something for me in the post. I waited excited as she got the letter out of a drawer. Then I saw my own handwriting "Pte. R. Baker" and his number, that and the address crossed out and above them was written, "Missing, believed killed."

I can't describe how I felt. I didn't know whether to believe he'd really gone or not. I couldn't not see him again, *I couldn't.*

A fortnight later my second letter was returned with that deadly sentence above my crossed-out writing. Then my third letter. This was worse than having all of them returned in one packet

I'd been brought up to take whatever came to me and that was all I could do now. So when I heard Fred was coming on leave I met him as usual. I told myself Ron was only believed killed and I'd heard of men sometimes turning up after that had been reported. You often heard stories about them being shell-shocked, losing their memories but being all right in the end.

The first Thursday in October there was Fred at the back door, freshly shaved, smart and upright as ever, but I realise now that he looked pitiful that day, marked by the trenches. As usual he brightened when he saw me. I knew I meant to him what Ron meant to me, but I was full of my own troubles and had a job even to smile. We walked into Newbury and had some tea. Fred could see I wasn't myself.

"What's up, Win?"

"Nothing, just a bit tired."

'Course I couldn't tell him and I never would.

Dear Fred was as cheerful as ever, never said anything about what he'd been through. Nothing, for instance, about his "mob" having to march day and night with hardly a break to take up the positions the French had run away from when they mutinied that year.

Nor about the nightmare of the duckboards. The only way to get the men from one place to another over the mud was with these boards. Because it had to be done in the dark dozens of them missed their footing and were sucked in and drowned. Once Fred heard a scream and knew it was one of his mates — a lad he'd known at school — but he didn't dare try to pull him out or he'd have gone too, and they'd been ordered not to stop for anything.

Nor about how he and some of the lads went out one night before going "over the top" and got blind drunk on rum, and how the next day when they went into action he could hardly put one foot before another, his brain wouldn't work properly. If you wasn't absolutely on the alert like you'd been trained to be you were a target. Fred saw a lot of them killed that day. It shocked him so much he made up his mind never to touch another drop before a battle. And he never did.

He could've told me what it was like to be gassed, get back to base with streaming eyes, throat all choked, unable to speak

97

and hardly able to breathe. And no sick leave after the gas because he was needed, as a trained soldier, to help the new ones that'd only just come out and didn't know anything, young officers and all.

If Fred had told me any of these things I'd have understood better than most because I remembered all those mock battles on the Plain — the smoke, the shooting, the barbed wire. I had some idea of what a battlefield must be like.

It was more than ten years later that I heard what it had been like for Fred and the others. That day in Newbury he just said we should go to the pictures because Mary Pickford was on and she was all the rage.

Although I was so miserable it was comforting to be with Fred again. Again I cried when we said goodbye — for Fred — for Ron — for all of them — and a bit for myself too.

I went on hoping I'd hear from Ron.

Highclere Castle, about 1900

In 1918 the Burtons made a big change. The Speen house was too small and they moved to Lomgmore Place, quite a grand house the other side of Newbury, with a beautiful garden, a tennis court and a big orchard. I can remember baskets and baskets of fruit being brought into the kitchen and Cook always making jam.

Now we were nearer the town I began to meet nannies from Highclere Castle, when we were all out with the children. Highclere was the Earl of Caernarvon's place. He was the one that found that tomb in Egypt some years[15] later. I remember the servants from Highclere talking about how he'd dug up a lot of treasures and saying they didn't think it was right to disturb the dead like that.

When I had to take our children to Highclere — what a performance! First you had to have a permit to go through the grounds, then take the children in the side door and up to the nursery where the children of the house were with their nanny. Take off their boots, put their little slippers on, brush their hair, remind them to behave: "Say 'please' and 'thank-you' and mind your noise." Up would come the parlourmaid to say Her Ladyship was ready and then the lady's maid would take them down to the drawing-room.

Having tea in the servants' hall I learned about the different ranks in the service world. One department was the butler's. He was in charge of the footmen and all the menservants in the house, except the valet. The housekeeper was very high up, directly under Her Ladyship and responsible for paying the women's wages. Under her, cook was head of the kitchen and over the housemaids, kitchenmaids and scullerymaids. The linenmaid and parlourmaid came under the housekeeper but not the lady's maid or the nursery people. If there wasn't a nursery governess there would be a head nanny, an under nanny to keep the pram and cots clean and tidy and a nursery maid to clean the nurseries.

I kept clear all my service life of upper servants. They were very jealous of their position and couldn't bear you to be in touch with the Lady or the Master. Even at East Grafton there was that business of the Cook not letting me see Mrs. Gauntlett, and in places where there was a bigger staff it was much worse.

Another thing housekeepers did in places like Highclere was to keep the under-servants without money. They were supposed to pay them, but sometimes the money went into their own pocket. They would tell the maids they were getting food and lodging and their training and that was the payment for their work. One kitchenmaid I knew had a young man in the town and when they found out, the housekeeper and cook, they kept her in, wouldn't let her go out and meet him in case she talked about not being paid and it got back to The Lady. Then there was another kitchenmaid, poor little soul, I think she came from the North, she never got a wage. The cook said she was learning her trade, she never gave her nothing, and then one day she was found drowned in the canal. There was an inquest and some mystery about it. I got a shock when I read it because I knew the place she come from. That's why I never wanted to work in big houses with a lot of upper servants. You never could trust them.

I had another friend in Newbury who wasn't in service. I met her through Dolly Adams, the girl with the Donnington Castle grandparents who'd known Ron. Dolly's friend was Maisie Stone, older than me and she worked at Camp's Drapery Bazaar, a department store in Northbrook Street — it's still there. Maisie was an overseer and she told me they were very short of staff because everyone was leaving to go into munitions. As I didn't like service and was interested in making clothes and especially in trimming hats, why didn't I join her at Camp's Drapery Bazaar and help with doing alterations? I could share her digs, it would be lovely for us. I was as keen as mustard to do this, but once again I had to ask Mother of course. You can guess what she said. Off went a letter to Mrs. Burton. On no account was she to accept my notice. All Win would be doing would be walking the streets of Newbury, and it full of troops!

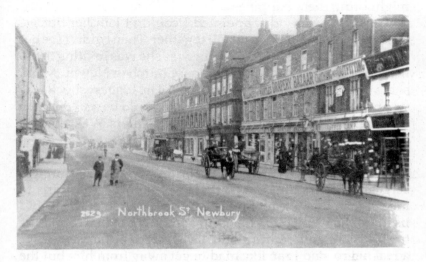

Camp's Drapery Bazaar, about 1908

When Mrs. Burton got Mother's letter she was very surprised.

"How could you think of leaving us, Winifred? And where would you live in Newbury, a young girl like you. (I was nearly nineteen). Your mother's quite right — you'll be much safer here with us."

She meant to be kind and keep an eye on me for Mother, but I do think she also had no intention of losing a good maid. So I didn't get my freedom and it was the same when I suggested going into munitions, something that would have been much better paid. I was kept down time and again by Mother who always seemed to be standing there like a big watchdog I couldn't get past. But I know how she felt and that she only meant to protect us. She'd had bad experiences herself when she was young and she couldn't see things any other way. But after the war thousands of women like me refused to go back into service, and many of them did get better jobs and more independence. And when some of us had daughters of our own we vowed we wouldn't stand between them and what might bring them happiness.

Maisie was very disappointed I couldn't join her but we kept in touch and often went out together. Then I didn't see her for a while and then the next thing was she was inviting me to her wedding. It was at St. Nicholas' Church in Newbury and some of the maids I knew were there. The biggest shock was when I saw the bridegroom. I knew he would be a soldier, the only men we girls was interested in was soldiers. Well, this one was very tall and *coal black*! Afterwards there was a big do at the church hall, arranged by her parents. There was wine and dancing. I seem to remember the bridegroom was wearing a sergeant major's uniform. Well, it was so new to us girls to meet a man that wasn't English, the fascination of it. He told us in fun he wanted to kiss us all and he chased us round the table, kissing anyone he caught. I was scared — he was so *BIG*, a real negro, and I ran like mad to get away from him but the others were shrieking away and enjoying it.

I didn't see Maisie again until she made the dress for my own wedding.

Marriage seemed to be in the air just then. The next thing I heard was that Dolly Adams had married her cousin the Australian, Ron's friend. I was glad I hadn't been asked to go but it seemed I couldn't escape Australians and weddings. On my next home holiday Mother and I went over to Collingbourne and Nell dragged us down to the church to throw confetti on a couple. The girl's name was Alice Roberts and, wouldn't you know, the bridegroom was an Australian, in the cavalry.

As it happened, that marriage had a sad end. After the war, when Alice and her two children sailed to Australia to join her husband he never turned up to meet them off the boat. I don't know the ins and outs but they had to come back to England. When Mother heard about that, she had a field day: "Look what happens when girls marry these Australian soldiers they don't know nothing about ..."

The little gold brooch Ron gave me had disappeared and I never saw it again.

Everyone was getting worn down, low spirited. Food was rationed now and there were queues everywhere. Then in spring, 1918 came the first of the 'flu epidemics and thousands died all over the country. There wasn't any of the drugs we have now to treat infections and I remember we had to watch little Pauline carefully because she was still very delicate.

We'd heard about the Russian Revolution in 1917, and now came the news that the Bolsheviks had shot the Czar, King George's first cousin. They said the King cried when he heard and he ordered Court mourning and a memorial service. The *Daily Chronicle* said the Czar had begged for his wife and children to be spared but in the end they killed the whole family.

The papers were beginning to say we were winning the war and there was talk about "What Women Will Want Now", reporters praising women's war work and saying they could never go back to doing just housework. That idea didn't last long I'm afraid.

The end was in sight but there was a lot about when and how to have an armistice. Meanwhile Fred and his pals had gone back for what the generals called "one last push". How did they stand it? As I see it now they were butchered and sacrificed for nothing.

November 7th, 1918 was my Thursday half-day. Down in the town I couldn't understand what was happening. Absolutely everyone seemed to be in the street, rushing about excited and trying to buy newspapers but the newsboys kept selling out. I managed to look at someone's paper: "The Great War nears its end. Armistice expected this week." So that was it. I caught the excitement and tried to push forward to hear more. Then I realised I'd lost my hat in the crush. I tried to get back down the street to look for it but just couldn't get through. I was swept along whether I wanted or not. It was frightening. The crowd was extra thick near the corner of Bartholomew Street where there was a little shop kept by an elderly German. He hadn't been interned but he was always watched and had to report to the police every week. Then I saw several men push into his shop. They came out dragging the poor man and carried him away. I don't know what happened to him. There was a lot of singing — "It's a long way to Tipperary", "Pack up your Troubles", "Keep the Home Fires Burning" — everyone waving, clapping, cheering, some of them drunk I suppose. I joined in the singing for a while but when I saw a space in the crowd I edged my way out and went back to Longmore Place.

Four days later, on the morning of November 11th we looked out and saw several aeroplanes. To see even one was a novelty in 1918 and everyone was at their windows. It was a misty day but we could gradually make out they were flying streamers, on them written: "Armistice signed: It's all over!" A newspaper headline said "Kaiser abdicates and Crown Prince goes with him."

On November 12th the papers were full of what was happening in London:

"'We want the King!' Crowds' thunderous cheers."

"Day of overflowing joy! Flag-waving babies."

"Lights of London for the gladdest day in Britain's History."

And they reported how the news of the Armistice came by telegraph to the newspaper offices. "10.27 Press Statement. The Armistice is signed and hostilities are to cease on all fronts at 11 am today."

We were happy and thrilled and so were our employers but they celebrated on their own. Even on Armistice Day is was "Us and Them." That's how it was Yesterday.

But Mrs. Burton must have had some bitter thoughts. A few days later Colin told me, "Mummy's very sad — Uncle Alec's been killed." She'd already lost one brother in the fighting and then they heard this one had died just one hour before the Armistice. I don't remember any more Christmasses at the grandparents' house because Mrs. Burton's poor father went mad after losing his second son. He died in an asylum.

But peacetime ways came round again. The Burtons began to live with more style. He had a car now, for work and family outings, only a little one, a Ford, but any car at all was something in those days. I loved going in it.

Then they started giving weekend tennis parties at Long-more Place. Mr. Burton was a good player and very keen. Sometimes they arranged matches in aid of charity. Cook had to prepare the refreshments and I watched her pressing tongues and beef, making trifles and summer pudding, laying it all out on tables under the trees. One day they even had the famous French tennis star, Suzanne Lenglen there playing for charity. I don't remember what she looked like but somehow I ended up having one of her racquets — I don't know how on earth that came about but I still have it in my attic today.

Sometimes at these gatherings I'd be there looking on, not in my uniform, and some of the gentlemen might talk to me. But as soon as they found out you were a maid that was the end and that used to make me mad. But there was one man that did stay interested in me for a long time. He was an army officer cousin of Mrs. Burton's called Peter something, about twenty-one, tall, brown-haired and good-looking. I remembered him coming to visit during the war after he'd been wounded, and now he took to coming up to the nursery and joining in my romps with the children. One day I said, "Is it the children or me you come to see?"

He grinned and said, "How about meeting me in Newbury this evening?"

I supposed it was all right and I did meet him once or twice, but of course he never told Mrs. Burton. He told me his family had lost all their money and there was a rich girl they wanted him to marry. Her father had been a rag-and-bone man before the war but then he went in for scrap metal for shells and made thousands. Peter couldn't stand the girl.

One day he said, "I'd like to marry you though. I'm thinking of going to Kenya — my uncle's there — to make a living. How about coming with me?"

"No! I don't want people looking down on me because I've been a servant."

"No-one would know in Kenya."

"Oh, yes they would. It'd all leak out, and you'd be asked

everywhere and I'd be shunned, I know."

He must have realised it would never work. Of course I liked him taking me out, but I didn't really care about him, certainly didn't love him.

I didn't love Fred either, or not in that way, but he was the one man Mother didn't mind me seeing and I was tired of fighting her. So when his next leave came and he asked if I could put two half-days together to go and stay a night with his family at East Grafton I asked Mrs. Burton for permission. Yes, she said. (She thought Fred was all right too.)

That Saturday evening Fred met me at Savernake station and took me to his home.

The Graces had been through cruel times ever since Fred's mother died in childbirth, a thing that upset Fred desperately as a lad of eleven. And their luck never changed — illness and poverty and early deaths; all Fred's five brothers died young and those that married had no children. His sister Emily was supposed to look after the home but she wasn't very bright and couldn't manage it properly. Bessie, his elder sister, had worked since she was thirteen for a Captain and Mrs. Wilberforce Bell. It was rough work, but Captain Wilberforce Bell did try to help the Graces by paying for bread to be delivered to them regularly. But the baker was a mean, dishonest man and he often made them pay for a loaf although he'd already had the money. Emily didn't dare say anything in case he stopped delivering. She'd had no education and didn't know how to stand up for herself. Fred's Dad was a bit the same but a very religious man and devoted to his children. But somehow people in the village seemed to look down on the Graces because they were poor and unlucky.

So — here I was visiting them this weekend. Mr. Grace and all of them were very nice and I could see that an "understanding" was growing about me.

In the morning we went to church but first we took a walk by the canal. Fred pointed out the willows growing beside the towpath.

"They'll soon be cutting them again to make cricket bats

Emily Grace at East Grafton

now it's peacetime. Down there's where they load the barges, but look Win, here's a special place I want to show you."

I followed him through a gap in the hedge, and was suddenly dazzled by a mass of blue. "Bluebells I gather," sang Fred and there they were, bluebells in their hundreds under the trees, with now and again a clump of primroses. He loaded some into my arms and put his arms round me and the flowers.

"I'm a man now, Win, like the song says."

As we went into church I looked towards the front left-hand pew where I'd sat with Millie and Cook five and a half years before. Fred led me to a seat at the back. I opened my book at Morning Prayer. Fred whispered "Turn over." Wondering why, I did so. "Turn over," he repeated, and as I turned to Evening Prayer, "further on, further on", went on the whispers, and I leafed through the Litany, Collects, Epistles, Gospels. The hand next to mine turned more pages for me: Communion, Baptism — and then I cottoned on. The hand stopped at Solemnisation of Matrimony.

"Read it through during the sermon."

When everyone settled down for the sermon I obediently read through from "Dearly beloved brethren, we are gathered together ... Holy Matrimony ..." through to the blessing, Fred watching. As we stood for the final hymn, I found myself whispering, "When do you want all this to happen?"

"Tell you next time I'm home," and he never mentioned it for the rest of that visit. Was I engaged? I supposed I was.

Fred's leaves were more often now the war was over and one day early in 1919 he came up to Longmore Place and found me fussing round the kitchen, cutting the bread-and-butter for the children's tea and making sure I'd done everything. Fred got impatient and said it was time we were out.

"Just a minute, I got to fill the hot water bottles."

"But it's s'posed to be your half-day!"

At last we got out and he told me his plans. He'd just come

East Grafton football team, early 1920s;
Fred 2nd. from right, middle row

from the Wiltshire regiment headquarters on Salisbury Plain. He'd been interviewed and medically examined with a crowd of other regulars (it was the regulars he'd joined in 1915) that had done so many years' service. If they were fit enough they had the chance to go out to Hong Kong and India with the regiment for another four years. It was to build them up after all the fighting, with good food, lots of sport and exercise. They'd be treated like heroes and given plenty of free time and no drilling or hard slogging. I suppose they thought these men would stay on in the army after that. But meanwhile it was a chance for Fred to see the world and rest his nerves a bit.

"Would you be willing to wait four years for me? If not, I won't go. We could be married as soon as I come back."

I could see he was keen to go and I thought why not, he

deserved it; and I wasn't in any hurry to get married. The ruby and diamond ring was the prettiest in the shop, but it cost three pounds. Fred said I was to have it.

He sailed for Hong Kong in September 1919 but first we told Mother and Dad we were engaged. I reminded Mother I'd be twenty-four by the time Fred got back. She'd taken Fred and me for granted for some time now, but on the quiet, without telling me, she made him promise that he'd come out of the army after the four years — he must never take me into that life. She was still deadly against soldiers and that would include Fred if he stayed in. He loved the army, in spite of all the horrors he'd seen; he loved the discipline and the smartness. But he promised.

Sister Nell and the other women around Collingbourne and East Grafton that had known Fred and me thought I was mad to marry a man that wouldn't have a job after he came out. They never said anything to me about that but gossiped away behind my back. Why didn't I marry a smart chauffeur or a valet that had a good secure job? Well, I didn't want none of those smooth fellows that thought themselves so much above the other servants.

And I never trusted them. Look what happened when I was friendly (just friendly, I was engaged after all) with a Highclere valet. This would be 1921 or '22. There were four brothers, two working in Highclere grounds, Reg the youngest was Lord Caernarvon's valet and the other brother was head game-keeper. He and his wife lived in the woods and I often used to visit them. Reg often seemed to call when I was there and I got used to seeing him on Thursdays and him walking back to Longmore Place with me in the evening.

One week I got a note saying he couldn't see me next Thursday because he had to go to London with the family. So I decided not to go up to Highclere but spend the afternoon in Newbury for a change. I was having tea in the usual cafe and in came a housemaid from Highclere.

"You won't be meeting Reg today, " she said.

"I know. He had to go to London."

"Elsie, (the lady's maid), she's gone too."

"I know."

"Bet you don't know they sleep together whenthey're away."

That was enough. I never went near Highclere again. 'Course I realise now the housemaid wanted him for herself. Service! It could be a crafty, sly, backbiting world. Oh, Mother had been right, I thought, to warn me against menservants. I'd stick to Fred. He wasn't Ron, and he wasn't special for me in the way I was for him, but he was faithful and good and he needed me. I ached with pity and admiration for him and all the thousands like him who'd been through that war to make a better world, so they thought, for us back at home.

1923 and I was leaving Longmore Place. Fred was back from Hong Kong with yards of white silk for my wedding dress and he'd be waiting at Collingbourne Station.

In the kitchen I pulled off my white cap, opened the stove door and threw it in. Cook gaped.

"What'n earth are you doin'? You'll be wanting that again."

"No, never." And I never did wear one again.

Mrs. Burton was very sad about me going and couldn't bring herself to see me off at the station, so her husband took me in the car, thanked me for my eight years and put me into a carriage with some magazines for the journey. I felt very smart in my navy blue costume with white silk blouse, white gloves and little hat with a curly white feather.

At Collingbourne there was Fred waiting excitedly with the trap. And who should be on the other platform talking to the station master but sister Nell, just back from Andover.

"Who's that young lady talking to Fred over there?"

"That's my youngest sister."

"Wh- a - a - t?"

"Yes, and she's gone and give up a lovely job and all the nice young men she could've had, just to marry him. How could she be so silly .... and he've got no job or anything ...."

Wedding Day 1924

NOTES

[1] The 'Bakes' are a feature of this part of Wiltshire. Among many others are Netheravon Bake, Rolston Bake and Compton Bake. The name is thought to have originated in the distant past when pieces of land were broken up with mattocks and burnt, with their remnants of vegetation, to produce potash for enriching the soil.

[2] This was actually Mr. Hungerford Athol Colston, later Lord Roundway. The title was not created until 1915.

[3] Cattle sheds

[4] a kind of porridge

[5] Probably Marie Stopes, who wrote *Wise Parenthood* in 1918.

[6] to make hay into a cock.

[7] Chaff and refuse left after threshing.

[8] Captain Scott's ill-fated Antarctic expedition of 1910-12

[9] Richard Jefferies, in his book *The Toilers in the Field*, 1892, remarks of middle-class farmers: "They do not ... at all relish the idea of sending their boys to the national school of the parish ... It has a faint suspicion of the pauper. Attempts have been made to get over this niceness by erecting a special class-room for farmers' sons." It is interesting to find this precedent for segregation being followed, on a different level, about fifteen years later at Everleigh School.

* In his *Plain Soldiering*, N.D.G.James refers to the early aviator, Horatio Barber, who in 1909 rented a piece of land at Larkhill. "On this site he arranged for a shed to be built in which he housed his new aeroplane when it arrived in June 1909." Soon the War Office was involved, further buildings

were erected, and developments began which led to the formation of the Royal Flying Corps in 1912. It seems likely that Winifred's dash to Larkhill took place somewhere between these two dates.

[11] yeast

[12] This historic building once functioned as a coaching inn on the London to Bath run. W.A.Edwards in *Everleigh: some notes on its story*, mentions sportsmen frequently gathering at the Crown for both hawking and hare coursing.

[13] Daughter-in-law to the Gauntlett Nell worked for.

[14] Winifred does not enlarge on this point. Does she mean annually or monthly? G.E. Mingay in his *Rural Life in Victorian England* describes South Wiltshire as the nadir of poor farm wages in the late nineteenth century. Government papers for 1898 bear this out and although they refer to a period rather more than ten years before
Winifred's, it appears that wages changed very little before 1914. Parliamentary Papers for 1899 on the Wages of Indoor Domestic Servants indicate that Winifred's and Millie's earnings were well below the national average. My very speculative estimate of Manor Farm weekly wage account, based on the above writings and Winifred's testimony, excludes day labourers and possible payments in kind. I think it is safe to assume that the annual account fell between three and four hundred pounds a year (*see opposite*)

Estimated Wages

Indoor Staff	Weekly Wages
Nursery governess	9/6d
Cook	9/3d
Housemaid/parlourmaid	1/-
Houseboy	4/-
Nursemaid	1/-
	£1.4.9.

Outdoor Staff

1st groom	14/-
2nd groom	5/-
Head carter	13/-
Under carter	11/-
3rd carter	5/-
Head cowman	13/-
2nd cowman	7/-
3 milkers @ 4/-	12/-
Poultrykeeper	4/-
3 shepherds @ 13/-	39/-
	£6.3.0.

Total weekly wages bill: £7.7.9. (estimated)

Total annual wages bill: £384.15.0. (estimated)

[15] Tutankhamen's, 1922

Winifred and baby Pauline

POSTSCRIPT

Winifred may have burned her cap and apron in 1923 but she hadn't seen the last of service or of hard times. At the age of fifty-three she found herself again looking after rich people's children, this time at a big country house in Buckinghamshire. After these children had grown up, she was kept on part-time to clean, make fires and beds and be on call for emergencies, as the smooth running of the house might require. Fred took a job as a gardener and they lived in a tied flat on the estate. After Fred's health forced him to retire, Winifred worked on until she was seventy-one.

In their earlier married years, the Graces struggled against illness, bad luck and disappointment. Poverty constantly threatened and Fred's mental health, apparently damaged in boyhood by the shock of his mother's early death, seems to have been virtually wrecked by his war years. Devoted to his wife, he worked hard when he was able but it was her determined optimism that kept them going.

Forbidden by Winifred's mother to stay in the army and disappointed in an attempt to emigrate, Fred found that farm work was still very much a hirer's market. Like many workers of their day, he and Winifred were often obliged to move their home to keep in employment, in their case five times. Their story, moving on a personal level, also demonstrates the appalling harshness of many lives, particularly in rural areas, before the coming of the welfare state. There were Trade Unions, but employers often found ways of outwitting them. Winifred gives examples:

At Devizes the Union men came round and said Fred was working far too many hours for his money. After a while they got an extra two shillings for cowmen, but Fred never gained anything because the farmer put our rent up. The Union fought again and got two more rises, but after the first our free milk was stopped, and after the second our permission to gather wood for the winter was taken away. You was never any better off.

Before the National Health Service was introduced in 1948, people unable to afford medical treatment frequently neglected illness and injuries, often with serious consequences. Winifred's sister Jane mistreated a septic toe with a resultant chain of disasters ending in gangrene, amputation of the leg and eventual death. Certainly the remote situation of many farm cottages made it difficult to seek treatment even for those who could afford it. For Winifred, though, a journey of any length was better than toothache.

I woke with a raging pain the right side of my face. Fred was going to be away all day haymaking. I thought Right! I'll go to Savernake (Hospital) and have it out. I went on my bike to Collingbourne, train from there to Marlborough, walked up the long hill to Savernake. I had the tooth out, the last person to go in the operating theatre that day. Almost as soon as I come round from the anaesthetic they turned me out. I walked down the hill, kept nearly collapsing from the ether stuff, got to Marlborough station and passed right out. The station master's wife gave me some brandy; she was worried about me but I got on the train, still smelling of this ether. At Collingbourne station I met a friend; she said I was in no state to ride that bike so she found someone — it was a lad I'd been to school with — to take me home. I was still bleeding and it was all over my coat, my hat and dress — such a pretty dress it was. When I got home I thought I must get Fred's supper, so I cooked some fish, put it in the oven, laid the table, all the time nearly passing out again, put the kettle on, made up the fire and thought 'Now I can go to bed.' When Fred came home, he saw a bowl of bloody handkerchieves in the larder and couldn't find me, so he went all round, to Mother's, to Jane's and all round looking for me. At last he came home worried to death but luckily I'd come round properly and got up by then.

Savernake Hospital

At the time of her one and only confinement Winifred was living at Beach's Barn, between Coombe Bake and Jane's home. She met the onset of labour with her characteristic stoicism and independence.

Unhappily the midwife's technique was so rough and primitive that it left Winifred weak and ill. Nevertheless Baby Pauline, named after little Pauline Burton, was a great joy to Winifred and Fred.

Not long after the horrific confinement Fred succumbed to

one of his many bouts of illness, refusing to leave his bed and unable to earn their living. He received some pay for six weeks but after that they had only their savings. After six months the day came when they were down to their last ninepence. That morning a gypsy called.

She was very tall and dark, Spanish-looking with huge gold earrings, a long black skirt and a red and black band round her forehead — a real Romany. I said, 'I'm sorry but I'm poor as what you are — we've got no money.' 'Well,' she said, 'You got some plum jam in your cupboard, give me a jar, and some potatoes and a cabbage from the garden — we've got a rabbit stew on. I'll give you two dozen of clothes-pegs for that.' Then she said, 'Well, my dear, I know you're in deep trouble but it'll all be over in four days. By the end of the month you'll be gone from here.'

A few days later Mrs. Burton, Winifred's old employer, acting on an intuition, called to see the Graces. Remembering her own father's mental breakdown, she was very sympathetic, and encouraged Fred to take a job with a farmer she knew at Aldermaston. Winifred inherited her mother's belief in the magical power of gypsies and even today she sees their hand in Mrs. Burton's timely visit and the happy years at Aldermaston that followed it.

These were the Grace's best years but they were interrupted by World War II. Then in his early forties, Fred had to choose between military service as a drilling sergeant or "essential work" on a larger farm as part of the war effort. He couldn't bring himself to train men to fight in another war so was directed to a large farm in Devizes.

Winifred's practical and resourceful attitude to life did not prevent her from nurturing occasional dreams and fantasies. During their time at Devizes she heard that Australian troops were at Tidworth. One night she dreamed that Ron was with them, fighting in this second war.

them, fighting in this second war.

Plain as plain, I saw him in my dream, marching along and looking just like he used to, and looking at me. I woke up very excited — I'd always thought I might see him again. When Fred had gone to work and Pauline to school, I got on my bike to Devizes, took the 'bus to Upavon, then a 'bus to Amesbury and from Amesbury to Tidworth. There *were* a lot of Australians in the town and I walked round and round until it was time to get the 'bus back, hoping and hoping I might see him. Then I came to my senses and felt very sad. I was perfectly happy with Fred, but if Ron had ever turned up ..... well, that's love, no-one can explain it.

But Fred was the reality in her life.

I never knew when he might refuse to go to work, take to his bed for weeks. I never bore a grudge because I remembered how he suffered in that war, what he did for his country and for all of us. When I did visit him in the mental hospital during his breakdowns he did walk down the ward with me when it was time to go, and the nurses called us the two lovebirds.

Despite his illnesses, Fred, cherished by his wife, lived to be almost eighty. He died in 1975. Some years later Winifred was almost crushed by the sudden death, in tragic circumstances, of their daughter Pauline. The cruelty of this seemed likely to overwhelm her, but her never-failing courage and some deep inner strength helped her to go on living.

Those of Winifred's sisters who survived into their seventies made up for their endless years of child rearing and backbreaking toil by dropping into armchairs and doing nothing, once those times were past. Their baby sister, who always thought there was more to life than cleaning and polishing, never lost her desire for action and knowledge. Always concerned for the welfare of her immediate neighbours, she now takes a lively interest in national and world events, having recently written to her M.P. on the plight of the homeless. If she hears of any injustice or malpractice, particularly on matters of farming, the treatment of animals or children, the appropriate authority will be sure to get a letter from her.

She passes her time in quiet busyness in the flat provided by her last employers, cultivating her garden, talking to visitors and ministering to the needs of an eighteen-year-old tabby cat. In May 1989 she celebrated her ninetieth birthday in some style, surrounded by friends and her two cherished grandchildren. Some months later a first great-grandson arrived to add to her joy.

I have a final comment on Fanny Spencer, Winifred's formidable mother.

From her Winifred inherited fortitude, self respect and immense will power. They were both spirited and resilient. Interviewed in her nineties, Fanny Spencer told a reporter how she started work at the age of eight. Her father's Dorset employer had issued the familiar ultimatum — the child must help on the farm or the family be evicted. She agreed to help with the cows but dared to ask for a wage of eightpence a day, which she got.

In the brutal school of Victorian rural poverty, physical strength was necessary for survival. To these Fanny added an iron moral code. She does not seem to have had Winifred's sense of fun or the compassion called forth by Winifred's wider experience. Yet there is ample evidence of her capacity for unsentimental kindness to her neighbours.

Her harsh treatment of the pregnant Annie reflected the harshness of society with its pitiless and often hypocritical judgments. She showed her concern for Annie many years later in Annie's luckless life. After eventually marrying a widower, Annie found herself drudging to support a family of nine, her husband made violent and unfit for work by an accident. It was then her mother who tackled the authorities insisting they give compensation and support.

An overbearing mother, but a faithful and ultimately a humane one, Fanny Spencer remains the profoundest influence on Winifred's life.

Fred and Winifred on holiday 1970s

Some other books from Ex Libris Press:

AUTOBIOGRAPHY

CHILD OF THE RED LION
An Hotelier's Story
'It is a beautifully written, warm, evocative memoir ...
great naturalness, humour and simplicity.'
Molly Maidment
135 pages; 18 photographs; Price £4.95

SEEDTIME TO HARVEST
A Farmer's Life
Arthur Court
'Arthur Court's autobiography is a thumpingly good
read, which anyone with even the slightest interest in
farming cannot fail to enjoy.'
126 pages; Map and photographs; Price £3.95

RALPH WHITLOCK

THE SECRET LANE
A Country Story
Set in the nineteen-thirties, this is the haunting story of
an enchanted summer in an English countryside that
has vanished forever.
151 pages; double page map; Price £4.95

LETTERS FROM AN ENGLISH VILLAGE
A Selection of articles from The Guardian Weekly
Illustrations by Roger Pearce

WILTSHIRE

CURIOUS WILTSHIRE
Mary Delorme
Photography by Duncan Skene
'A pot-pourri of some of the more interesting features of the Wiltshire landscape. The volume is well produced and contains a number of excellent photographs.'
159 pages; maps and photographs; Price £5.95

MISCELLANEOUS

GRAN'S OLD-FASHIONED REMEDIES, WRINKLES AND RECIPES
Jean Penny
Remedies for common ailments; wrinkles, or tips, to save time and effort about the house; recipes using inexpensive ingredients to create mouth-watering dishes: all are included within these pages.
94 pages; numerous engravings; Price £2.95

OUR NEIGHBOURLY GHOSTS
Tall and short stories from the West Country
Doreen Evelyn
Illustrations by Sarah Jonas
'Ghosts galore in this enjoyably spine-tingling collection.'
89 pages; Illustrated with pen and ink drawings; Price £2.95

Ex Libris Press books may be obtained through your local bookshop or direct from the publisher, post-free, on receipt of net price, at 1 The Shambles, Bradford on Avon, Wiltshire, BA15 1JS. Please ask for our free catalogue.